THE GANG ON KENDAL STREET

A FIFTIES MEMOIR
GROWING UP IN HENRY FORD'S HOMETOWN

by BOB BIERMAN

To my wife June, parents Adeline and Hank Bierman, brothers Jack and Tom, sisters Glenda Bruce and Patty Schenk, and the Kendal Street gang for their love, friendship and fond memories. And a special thanks to John Miller for his encouragement and editorial skills.

CONTENTS

AUTHOR'S NOTE

"When I was younger I could remember anything whether it happened or not, but I am getting old, and soon I shall remember only the latter."

Mark Twain

Several years ago I started jotting down on scraps of paper short reminders of my experiences as a youth growing up in a middle-class neighborhood in Dearborn, Michigan. By the time I retired in 1995 I had accumulated more than a hundred bits of childhood trivia and decided one day to organize and then expand them into short stories. Later, when I had finished the stories, I anticipated passing them along to my children so they would have a better understanding of my life as a young man. I was encouraged to do this after I videotaped an interview with my parents and learned so much about them and their life growing up on farms in Nebraska.

One year after I retired, I took a "Writing Your Memoirs" course at the University of Tennessee. For one assignment, I wrote and read to the class, "The Wrecking Crew," one of the chapters in this book. It was well received.

Encouraged, I decided to put the stories in the form of a book and have several hundred copies printed.

It has been a labor of love, reminiscing as I searched through old photographs, read yellowed newspaper clippings and old love letters, perused high school year books and long-forgotten grade school autograph books, and retrieved from the attic old trophies, varsity letters and sweaters, and other pieces of memorabilia.

The gang on Kendal Street was not a gang in the modern sense of the word, but simply a bunch of guys who, growing up, had a very close relationship. The only trouble was an occasional speeding ticket and some underage drinking. Our house was the unofficial headquarters. Friends were coming and going constantly. My parents always made them feel welcome, and several still drop in to say hello when they are in the neighborhood. The friendships established those many years ago have endured and are treasured.

This book covers a period from my childhood to my marriage in 1958. All of the incidents reported here are true, but the individuals involved may remember the details differently. The dialogue, in most cases, is a product of my imagination.

Bob Bierman

PREFACE

At a seminar sponsored by The Fountain Group, the president opened his remarks with a list of items that are common today but which were unknown when I was in grade school. Excerpts from his comments are printed here because they set the tone for the period covered by much of this book.

"We were born before television, before penicillin, before polio shots, frozen foods, Xerox, plastic, contact lenses and the 'Pill.' We were born before radar, credit cards, split atoms, laser beams and ball point pens, before pantyhose, dishwashers, clothes dryers, electric dryers, electric blankets, air conditioners and drip dry clothes."

"We got married first and then lived together. In our time, closets were for clothes, not for "coming out of." Bunnies were small rabbits and rabbits were not Volkswagens. We were before house husbands, gay rights, computer dating, dual careers and commuter marriages. We were before day-care centers, senior centers, group therapy and nursing homes. We never heard of FM radio, tape decks, electric typewriters, artificial hearts, word processors, yogurt and guys wearing earrings. Making out referred to how we did on our exam. Pizza, McDonalds and instant coffee were unknown."

"In our day, cigarette smoking was fashionable, grass was mowed, Coke was a cold drink, and pot was something you cooked in. AIDS were helpers in the principal's office. For one nickel you could ride a street car, buy an ice cream cone, make a phone call, buy a Pepsi or enough stamps to mail one letter and two post cards. You could buy a new Chevy Coupe for $600.00 and gas was 11 cents a gallon. For us time-sharing meant togetherness, not computers or condominiums. A "chip" meant a piece of wood, hardware meant hardware and software wasn't even a word."

While we have experienced substantial change in our lifetime -- some for the better and some not -- there are universal values that are timeless. Among them are good friends and the memories of good times with good friends. ◆

1

MY PARENTS

"At the end of your life you will never regret not having passed one more test, winning one more game, or not closing one more deal. You will regret time not spent with a husband, a child, a friend or a parent."

Barbara Bush at Wellesley

M y mother reached for a handkerchief tucked in her sleeve and started to cry. I was videotaping an interview with my parents and she was relating an incident that happened following a date in the tiny farm community of St. Ben, Nebraska, where she spent the early years of her life. She was just 17 at the time. We took a break.

1

I had suggested the interviews because I knew a time would come when it would no longer be possible to capture on tape the background of these two beautiful people. It was being done not so much for me as for my children, and their children, and their children. I wanted them to know

Mom on her 20th birthday

the hardships these people endured, their moral and ethical values, and what life was like for them growing up in the early 1900s. What I appreciated most was their stories about growing up. I never thought about my mother as a little girl playing with dolls, crying over a scratched knee, being teased by an older brother or afraid on her first day of school. And later, starting to wear makeup and getting excited about going on a date. And my father, crying as a child when his mother died, milking cows before dawn, smoking behind the barn, drinking his first beer, playing baseball, being disciplined by the nuns, or going to town for a dance. To me, they were always my grown-up parents.

My mother continued her story.

"My girlfriend Alvina and I were returning from a double date. As we turned off the dirt road and headed up the lane to my house, the headlights caught my father stepping from the wash house with a shotgun. He aimed at the car. We skidded to a stop. I stepped out of the car. The wheels spun in place momentarily, dust and stones flying, before

Mom (left) and her friend Alvina when they were nurse assistants in Columbus, Nebraska

the tires grabbed and my date made a hasty retreat leaving me to face my father's wrath.

I was in trouble, big trouble, and I knew it. My father had forbidden me to date this guy. His name was Duke, Duke Arlt. Duke was a bit wild, a free spirit whose speech was sprinkled with hell, shit and damn. I was caught disobeying my dad and I was going to suffer the consequences. He grabbed my arm and pushed me into the house."

She held her hands up to her face as tears again rolled down her cheeks. My mother is a very strong woman emotionally. She rarely cries.

"It was awful. The next morning I was told that I was not to leave the house for one year unless my mother or dad was with me. Today, I guess you would say I was grounded for a year.

"I really liked that guy," she said. At that, I looked at my father who turned his head toward my mother and with a laugh said, "I guess I was her second choice."

As it turned out, my mother served only three months of her "sentence" before she and Alvina accepted housekeeping positions in Amarillo, Texas. Even the parish priest was critical of her father for his harsh discipline. My grandmother apologized to my mother a few years later. It was much later, however, before my grandfather told my mother he was sorry about the incident.

My mother is the second oldest of 13 children and my father is one of 11. Large families were common then. Children were needed to work the farm. The Boesch family lived across the road from my mother and they had 14 children. My grandfather insisted he was not in competition with those folks across the road who were interested only in quantity. He sought quality, he claimed.

St. Ben is now nothing more than a dusty crossroads in central Nebraska. Although time hasn't exactly stopped here, it's certainly in no hurry. The only establishment is Arlt's Tavern, owned by my cousin Glenn Arlt. There also is a cemetery that dates back to the turn of the century. I have been there many times and have always found it fascinating. Walking with my mother, she would have a running commentary, "That's your uncle over there; here's your second cousin; that's your great aunt; that's Aunt Annie's little boy." What is so tragic and so sad about this cemetery is the number of babies buried there, some only two or three days old, and two or three children from the same family buried just a few days apart. Babies who died at birth and mothers who died giving birth are buried there. Often when a baby died the next child born of the same gender would be given the same name. My father, for example, had two brothers named Joe. The first one died when he was two years old. Dreaded diphtheria would sweep through small farm communities like St. Ben and leave half the population dead in its wake. There was no cure. Living was hard. Life was cruel.

A century ago the death of infants and young children was commonplace, especially in remote farm communities where there were few up-to-date medical facilities. My father's parents were not exempt from this tragedy. They were married in 1885 and had 11 children: Mary died at 18, Charlie at 3, Fred at 5 and Joe at 2. Of the seven surviving children, eight of their children died before the age of 10.

In the early 1900s there were some 80 people living in St. Ben. At that time there was a Catholic church, a Catholic school, a bar, a dry goods store and a gas station. Everyone who lived there was Catholic. The school had four rooms and went through the eighth grade. The nuns who taught there came from Germany. My parents walked one and one-half miles to school, up hill both ways, my dad would say with a smile. He said they would walk to school in the worst weather. Some days it was so bad they could get to the barn only by holding on to a rope that was strung there from the house. And if you don't believe me, he would say, I can still show you the rope in the garage.

According to my mother, she was the best speller and best reader in the class, but was poor at math. She boasted she was always the first to be picked for a spelling bee. She didn't say anything about her penmanship, but it is beautiful.

My father also had good penmanship, but he was not a very good student. His objective was to finish school and get on with his life. His mother had died of cancer when he was eight years old and he had been living with his sister Annie since then. Following graduation from the eighth grade, he worked on farms in Nebraska and Oklahoma.

In 1925, at the age of 19, he joined the Army Air Corps and was stationed at Kelly Field in San Antonio, Texas. He was a photographer's assistant there for two years when he decided that the military was not really his calling. He wrote to his brother Joe and asked for a loan of $125 so he could buy his way out of the Army. Joe sent the money. Dad spent the money. He never told me this, but I have heard that he took the money and went to see a lady friend in Colorado only to discover on his arrival that she had recently married a local boy. He returned to Kelly Field sad, broke and lonely. Several weeks later he wrote to his brother Bill asking for a loan of $125. He got the money and this time used it for which it was intended. He left the Army.

He and a friend hitch hiked to Jackson, Michigan, his friends hometown, hoping to find work. They didn't, and my dad returned to Nebraska where he again labored as a farm hand.

In August 1929 he and a friend drove to Toledo, Ohio, where they were told work was available at the Overland Car Company. It was only a rumor. The company was not hiring so they went on to Detroit to try their luck at Ford Motor Company. After a week there my father still had not found work and was nearly broke. He packed his bag and was walking out the door of his apartment when the landlady stopped him and insisted that he stay until he found work. Three days later, on August 12, 1929, he was hired by Sealtest Creamery. His starting pay was $25 a week. He worked there until he retired 42 years later. It was with this job that he began spelling Bierman with one n. Until then it had two.

Except for my mother's trip to Amarillo, she always worked close to home. She had to return home from Amarillo after seven months to help her mother who was pregnant with Kenny, her 12th child. Later she did housework and was a nurse assistant in Columbus, Nebraska. She met my dad there at a dance one Sunday evening. He was visiting from Detroit and they dated several times before he had to return. They corresponded and he eventually asked her to marry him. She accepted and took the bus to Detroit.

Before she left St. Ben, one of her girl friends had a wedding shower and asked everyone to bring a quarter. That was too much for some so they made an excuse and didn't attend. The Depression was at hand. The farmers were suffering. What crops the drought didn't get, the hoppers did, they said. My mother was grateful for the 12 quarters she received.

They were married in Detroit on June 5, 1933, at St. Leo's Catholic Church. My mother

recalls an incident that occurred shortly after the ceremony. My father thanked the priest who performed the ceremony and handed him $5. The priest looked at the bill, turned to my father and said, "You are the cheapest skate I ever did meet. I'm sure happy you're not marrying a St. Leo's girl."

There was no honeymoon. They lived in two or three rental homes and apartments before they had saved enough money to buy a home way out in

Dad, the best dressed man within 100 miles of St. Ben.

the suburb of Dearborn. They paid $375 for the lot and $4,250 for the home. That was in 1939. Mom still lives in that home on Kendal Street.

Mom was the boss in our household. She paid the bills and made the decisions. That seemed to be just fine with dad. He was a happy-go-lucky man who accepted life as it was presented. It was not his style to attempt to change any situation, but to adapt and make the best of it. He would never insist that things ought to be other than they were. Life was fine the way it was. He worked hard and never passed up an overtime opportunity. Likely something my mother encouraged.

She worked, too. She gave organ lessons for many years and also worked in the kitchen at the Howard Johnson's restaurant on Telegraph. Many nights I drove to pick her up when she finished work at 10 p.m. I had just received my license and volunteered to make the nightly run.

My parents were not big on pets. We never had any and I suppose it was because they felt the care and feeding of five kids was challenge enough without having a dog or cat around. My Uncle Elmer and his wife Carolyn had a dog for many years. Banjo was a cute, well behaved dog that my aunt and uncle worshiped and cared for as if it was their child. They never were blessed with children. One summer they asked my parents to watch Banjo for a few weeks while they vacationed in Colorado. Banjo was with us for only three or four days when he ran away. We searched for days and even posted reward posters throughout the area, but Banjo was never to be heard from again. I wasn't home, didn't want to be home, when Elmer and Carolyn returned from their vacation and rushed into the house to retrieve the dog they had missed so much. My mother had to explain that Banjo was gone. There was much wailing and knashing of teeth.

My sister Pat and her husband Gene had a cat with them when they drove from Florida to Dearborn for my father's funeral. While still in Dearborn, Gene suffered a mild heart attack and was hospitalized. Pat asked my mother to watch the cat while Gene was recuperating. Mom said she would, but the cat would have to stay on the screened-in back porch. She didn't care much for cats, or dogs for that matter. Later, she agreed to allow the cat to stay in the basement After a few weeks the cat was so well behaved my mother let her have the run of the house. When the time came for Pat and Gene to head back home to Florida they went by the house to pick up the cat. "Get your hands off that cat," mom shouted. "She's my cat now and she's staying here." My mother still has that cat. It has no name.

I never heard or saw my parents argue or have a serious disagreement. I know they had their occasional disputes because there were times when my dad would spend the night on the couch in the basement. He enjoyed a beer or two from time to time and that usually was the source of their spats. He never missed work, but I know there were times when he suffered mightily delivering milk after a long night at the bar. He was the kind of drinker who could go months without touching the stuff, but then one day after work he would stop at the Neighborhood, a bar near the Creamery, and have a drink with the guys. One was never enough. He knew he was going to catch hell and would be sleeping on the couch whether he got home at 9 p.m. or 2 a.m. so he often opted to stay until the place closed.

He usually made it home without incident, but there were two noteworthy exceptions. The first was when he ran into the back of a fire truck with its lights and siren on The other time was when he fell asleep in an open boxcar. When the train lurched forward, he awoke from his slumber and in a panic leaped into the darkness. He traded his train bed for a cinder bed, which he hit head first causing a small black cinder to be lodged in the bridge of his nose. That cinder remained there for the rest of his life, a constant reminder of that fateful night. Another reminder was his new nick name, "cinder nose." That didn't detract from his good looks.

I have been told that my father was a gifted athlete growing up in St. Ben. He played first base for the St. Ben team that traveled to other towns in the area for Sunday afternoon games. On one occasion when we were playing catch on the street with several neighbor kids, he casually mentioned that he played first base for several years with the Cardinals. I soon found out it was the St. Ben Cardinals he meant and not the St. Louis Cardinals, but several neighbors didn't know the truth until I revealed it during the eulogy at his funeral many years later. The only time I ever saw him play was at father and son games and that was hardly any test of his skills.

Dad was a sharp dresser who took pride in his appearance. He stood tall and straight and had

Dad (standing second from right) with the St. Ben Cardinals
baseball team

13

strong even teeth and big hands. He always ate heartily but never gained weight, remaining thin throughout his adult life. He reminded me a lot of movie actor Randolph Scott.

When my children were growing up, my wife June and I never missed a school activity in which they were involved, whether it be a Christmas concert, a play, talent show or athletic event. In fact, when we moved to the Cleveland area and our oldest son Todd remained in Dearborn for his senior year at Edsel Ford, we returned for every one of his football games and track meets. This was not unusual. Some fathers would even go watch football practice every day.

This is in total contrast to the involvement on the part of my parents in my school activities. My mother has never seen me play a single baseball or basketball game and my father saw only one basketball game. This was not unusual for the late '40s and early '50s. I didn't expect them to attend. Few parents did. They worked hard and little thought was given to watching us kids play games.

My mother is a petite, beautiful woman. She's a great cook and meticulous housekeeper who would be mortified to think there might be a dust mite lurking in some dark corner of the house. I knew from an early age that she had a beautiful singing voice. There was never a gathering of her family that they did not stand around the piano and sing. They harmonized beautifully. In later years they sang at the funerals of their brothers and sisters. They were introduced as the "Singing Diederich Family."

I did not know my father had a beautiful singing voice until he was well into his 60s. He learned the words to the George Burns song, *I Wish I Was 18 Again*. There was never a party after that when he was not asked to do his rendition. It has a beautiful melody, but I think some of the words are a bit sad:

> *I'll never again turn the young ladies heads*
> *I'm three quarters home from the start to the end*
> *Old oaks and old folks standing tall just pretend*
> *I wish I was 18 again*

Here is the eulogy I gave at my father's funeral. It says much about him and the kind of individual he was in life.

I have been asked to make a few comments about my father. He was born in 1906 and was one of 11 children. His name was Henry Conrad Biermann. At least that was what was on his birth certificate. He had many other names. To his five children he was Dad. He was Grandpa to his 16 grandchildren and Great Grandpa to his 16 Great Grandchildren. He also had a less endearing name some old-timers may recall — cinder nose.

When he was born, Bierman was spelled with a double n, but in the early 1930s my father dropped one n. It was no big deal, but we now get a lot of mail from the Rabbi at the Temple Beth El synagogue.

You won't find his name in Who's Who, but that's only because there is no Who's Who for a kind, gentle, loving and devoted father where his name would appear at the top of the list. During his life he was a farmer, ranch hand, photographer's assistant in the U.S. Army Air Corps, and a milkman. He enjoyed the Army about as much as I did — not much. In fact, in those days one could buy out of the service and my dad tried to do that twice. The first time his brother Joe sent him the money and after receiving it my dad thought the Army wasn't so bad after all and he and his buddies spent the money on a good time. Later, his brother Bill sent him the money and this time it was used for its intended purpose.

He was a patient man, but even his patience wore thin and he became exasperated trying to teach my brother, Jack, and me to drive that old stick-shift Pontiac.

He was an honest man, but was known to stretch the truth from time to time. I remember him playing catch in front of the house with me, Jack and some neighbor kids and claiming that he once played first base for the Cardinals. We later discovered it was not the St. Louis Cardinals, but the St. Ben Cardinals. St.

Ben is a dusty crossroads in central Nebraska where my father was born and raised.

He was a generous man. On more than one occasion our friends dropped by the house short of cash and looking for a quick loan. My father would go to the basement and return in a short time with the money. We never did find that loose brick that was his hiding place.

He was sneaky. When our house was quarantined because we had diphtheria, my father, against the health department rules, sneaked into the house one day. Shortly afterward the health department inspector arrived. Dad rushed to the basement and hid in the fruit cellar counting jars of canned tomatoes.

He was a hard worker. I do not recall his missing a single day of work in the 42 years he worked for Sealtest Dairies. He often volunteered to work overtime. He got that job during the Depression only a few days after he had packed his bags and was heading back to Nebraska broke. The landlady stopped him and told him he could stay rent free until he found a job.

In his early days delivering milk, he had a horse-drawn wagon. Dad called the horse Citation, but his real name was Doc. Doc was a good horse, knew every stop on the route, but had a mind of his own. Often my dad would return to the curb after a delivery only to see the horse trotting down the street on his way back to the barn.

17

My dad had a good sense of humor. I remember one incident that is particularly appropriate today. He was talking with Tom Bruce, my brother-in-law, and asked him if he would say something good about him at his funeral. He could not stop laughing when Tom responded, "Only if and when you do something good."

There are small, inconsequential things I remember about him. Dad on the couch watching TV, his long legs stretched out, his arm around me or tousling my hair. He never complained and accepted life as it was dealt to him, always grateful for the good things that came his way and forgiving when life seemed unfair. He was always upbeat.

I am fortunate to be part of a loving, caring, close-knit family, but over the past few days when I got to thinking how much my dad meant to me, I recalled, quite sadly, that I had never said "I love you."

Dad, I love you. ◆

2

OUR HOME

". . . said premises shall not be occupied by, leased or sold to any person or persons other than those of the Caucasian race."

Abstract of Title
Ford-Chase Subdivision No. 1
Recorded Oct. 29, 1935 10:11 a.m.

I t was 1939, during the Depression, when my parents took their life savings and invested in a home at 6030 Kendal in East Dearborn. It was their dream home, but they could never have imagined all the joyous, angry, humorous and sad moments they and their five children were to experience there over the next 60 years.

Our house on Kendal Street

FOR SALE

Immaculate Bungalow on Quiet Street
Three Bedrooms
One and 1/2 baths
Finished basement
Car and 1/2 garage
1,300 square feet

This is how a real estate agent might list the house. What it says is true, but for those of us who lived there it is so much more. Let me tell you a few things about this home that you would not get from a salesman.

Let's go in the back door. We never use the front door. Notice the basement stairway directly ahead of us. Well let me tell you a story about those stairs. It involves my Aunt Agnes who watched us kids for a few days when my parents were on a rare trip out of town. She slept in the bedroom on the other side of the bathroom. In the middle of the night, only half awake, she rolled out of bed and went to relieve herself. In the darkness she staggered in one bathroom door and out the other so she was standing right here with her back to these stairs. She pulled down her pants, lifted her nightgown and backed into what she thought was the toilet. She proceeded to take a seat. Now let me tell you that woman went ass-over-tea-kettle down those stairs, arms flailing and panties flying. The noise was something to behold. She was a-screaming and a-bouncing and a-rolling down those stairs until she got to the bottom where a quiet moan could be heard as she relieved herself. Amazingly she was not hurt and had only a few bruises.

On the stove here in the kitchen is the ceramic coffee pot with the Cook Coffee Company logo. That pot has been in this house for at least 45 years. Seems like things lasted longer in those days, especially if kept away from the kids. The huge cast iron skillet my mother kept in this stove drawer was missing one day. Later, we learned my brother

Jack used it on a picnic one Sunday morning to pound a horse shoe stake in the ground and punched a hole right through the middle. So much for things lasting longer.

My mother is a wonderful cook, but our dining area was pitifully lacking ambience. For many years our meals were served in the basement on a table that was originally our back porch. The top was linoleum and the legs were 4x4s.

The table with four chairs around it once seated seven after we moved from the basement to the kitchen for our meals. That chair against the wall by the heater vent was usually where I sat. I was home for lunch one day when I was in junior high school. Playing around, I picked up a glass of milk with my teeth and when I lifted my head the glass broke, fell from my mouth and sliced my wrist. A neighbor took me to the hospital where I had eight stitches. It was in this same kitchen a few years earlier when I was laid upon this table and told to count to ten while sucking in a dose of ether. I woke up an hour later less my tonsils and inhaling the pleasant aroma of Dr. Runge's Cuban cigar.

See that corner in the dining room? That's where my mother spilled a bottle of ink on her brand new carpet. It was a sad day. It was a day long before ball point pens were in common use. Of course, that carpeting is long gone. Also gone is the dining room table. It wasn't used often enough to justify the space it occupied. I missed it when it was gone. When my mother was angry with me she would chase me around that table wielding her hair brush and screaming for me to stop. I usually didn't, hoping in time she would cool down.

During World War II my mother put a small flag with five stars in that dining room window. It was the custom then to do this to show how many family members were in the Armed Forces. The Lindsay (Nebraska) Post carried a front page story on my mother's five brothers, labeling a picture of them, "The Five Fighting Diederich Democrats." The article, encased in plastic, still rests prominently on the dining room china cabinet.

The start of World War II was announced on a radio that sat in this corner next to the dining room. It was a tall Philco radio. I can still see my parents listening intently and pacing slowly as details of the Pearl Harbor bombing were being announced. The radio we listened to most often was in the basement. The entire family would sit there listening to such shows as the Lone Ranger, Jack Benny or Burns and Allen and stare at the radio like it was a television set.

Our telephone has always been on this dining room wall. It was and continues to be the only phone in the house. A call to a girl friend or boy friend could be overheard by all so conversations were somewhat bland. Our first phone number was

ORegon 8596. Later it was LUzon 1-8596. Then it went to 581-8596. The area code was added in 1952. My father won a 45 rpm record player at a Dairymen's Federal Credit Union party. It was kept on a dining room table beneath the window. We had very few records, the first two being *Too Young* and *Mona Lisa* by Nat King Cole. I can't help remembering my teenage years whenever I hear those songs

The organ was the focal point in the living room. My mother played often and also gave lessons. My second oldest son, Randy, was given lessons when he was so young he could not reach the pedals from the bench. He stood at the organ. When I was working at the Ford Rotunda and going to night school at Wayne State University, I would stop here between work and school and take lessons. Unfortunately, I quit after a few months.

The main-floor bedroom is where my brother Tom was born. My brother Jack and I were shipped off to our Aunt Maggie and Uncle Bill's farm in Utica, Michigan, so we would be out of the way. They lived in a small home and raised a large family. Some of the girls became nuns. I vividly recall waking up in the tiny kitchen to the smell and sound of bacon crackling on the stove and seeing a strip of sticky fly paper hanging from the overhead light.

We children slept in the two upstairs bedrooms. There was one bathroom up there for the five of us, but we managed with very few problems. One winter night I stood in the driveway and threw a snowball at our bedroom window. The light went on when the first one struck the window. When I threw the second one, it stuck against the window. I could hear my brother screaming as he bolted from the room and made it downstairs in three steps. I rushed in to explain that I, and not some intruder, was the culprit.

Five children were raised in this house, three boys and two girls. Jack is the eldest. I was born 16 months later and Patty Ann and Glenda followed in quick succession. There were four of us born in six years. Tommy came several years later. Many of our friends in the neighborhood spent more time in our home than they did in their own. They would not knock on the door or ring the bell, but would simply walk right in the back door like they were home. Until 10 years ago the door was never locked.

I came across two letters recently that I sent to my girl friend (later my wife), June Hopka, when she spent a week in Carlton, Michigan, with her cousin Carolyn. They were written in July 1952 and are interesting in what they reveal about our home as a neighborhood headquarters and my life at that time. Incidentally, each letter took a three cent stamp. Here are excerpts.

Hi Honey,   *July 23*
It's noon now and I have to umpire a game this afternoon at 12:30 so I won't be able to write very much. I just came back from baseball school. Johnny Pesky was there this morning.

Gary Gates and Tom Kovach just came downstairs where I'm writing the letter. Lynch just came down too. ..... I got a letter this morning from the Recreation Department telling me that I was chosen to play on the Dearborn All-Star baseball team. Our first game is against Plymouth on Friday afternoon. I have to work tonight at TenEyck at a band concert..... Well, it's 12:15 now and I have to be at Hemlock Park at 12:30 so I better close until tomorrow, honey, so good-bye.

Hi Honey,   *July 25*
Well, I just finished my morning game, and I have a half-hour yet before I start my afternoon game so I thought I'd write you a little bit now and finish it tonight. I have a baseball game tonight at Hemlock, but it probably will be a forfeit. I hope so. I'm so happy that I made the Dearborn All-Star team that I could die!! Pat McEvoy and Bob Simone were the only other players on our team to make it. We play tomorrow night. If we win I think we get to play at Belle Isle. Gates and Rooney are upstairs watching the convention. I think my mother should start charging them for room and board. They practically live here.

Jerry Lynch (right) shares a laugh with sister Glenda at our house while brother Jack (center) and Tom Okray look on.

Jim Rooney (left) and Gary Gates on the beach at Camp Dearborn in the summer of 1953

Jim Rooney teases brother Tom and sister Glenda.

I am reminded of how it was when I would go call on my friends. Call on them is what we did, literally. We would stand at the back porch and shout their name -- JER-REEE, DEN-NISSS, JI-IMM. Seems a bit odd to me now. It never occurred to us to knock on the door or ring the doorbell. Gary Gates was the exception. He lived with his mother on the second floor of an apartment building on Middlesex. We knocked there.

Our friends particularly enjoyed sleeping over. When our guests awoke in the morning and went downstairs to retrieve their shoes, they were pleasantly surprised to find that they had been polished. It was my father. Every morning before leaving for his milk route he would polish any shoes he found on the steps leading to our bedroom. What a nice thing to do. It was a random act of kindness long before the term appeared on bumper stickers.

Christmas was always a wonderful time. Like all young kids, we would rush downstairs early in the morning and find our treasures scattered throughout the living room. I never thought much about it at the time, but our gifts were never wrapped. No suspense here. What you saw is what you got.

I often think about one Christmas in particular. I was about ten years old and had gone to bed early on Christmas Eve. I couldn't sleep in anticipation of the next morning. Suddenly the bedroom light went on and my father walked in the room. He handed me a watch. "I'm sorry," he said, "but this is all we can afford for Christmas this year." When he left I cried. Surely he was kidding. There would be presents in the morning under the tree. There weren't. I should have been more understanding. My parents would often tell me that when they were growing up on the farm, they were thrilled to get an orange for Christmas.

Jack, mom and me, Christmas 1954

When I was in my senior year in high school we started having a party at our house on Christmas night. Word spread and before long it became a tradition. All of our friends and even a stranger or two would come by. There always was plenty of beer and food. At some point in the evening when our vocal cords had been sufficiently lubricated and our inhibitions had fled, my mother would sit down at the organ and we would all gather around and sing Christmas carols. It was a wonderful time.

The smell of a cigar in our home one Halloween night after I returned from begging was a sure sign that Dr. Runge had been there. I could hear my brother Tom's heavy breathing coming from the bedroom. My mother said the doctor had given him some medication and had diagnosed his ailment as diphtheria. Later the good doctor said that Tom would have died by morning had he not come by that night, and that a younger doctor probably would have had difficulty diagnosing the ailment. It was only a few years later that Tom was diagnosed with Perthies disease, a disease that inhibits hip growth. The treatment is to encase the hip and leg in a cast. Tom lived like this for 18 months with the aid of crutches which he often used as weapons.

The day after Tom had been diagnosed with diphtheria, the Health Department came by and put a large red 'Quarantine' sign on the front door. Nobody could come in the house and nobody could leave, except my father who was allowed to move out so he could continue working.

My brother Jack and I remained in good health and my sisters were only slightly affected. But there we were, confined to our house for what turned out to be 27 days.   For us, the house was the basement, except at night when we went upstairs to our bedrooms. My friend Jerry Lynch came up the alley once a week or so with comic books that he would hand to me over the fence. We all survived alright, but it was an experience we will never forget.

We were strict Roman Catholics. My brother Jack and I were altar boys, my sisters attended Catholic school, my mother sang in the choir and my father was an usher. When we said the name of Jesus we nodded our heads in reverence. Every evening during Lent we would kneel around the radio and pray the rosary. Missing mass on Sunday was a very serious offense. Divorce was out of the question. So was cremation. Fallen away Catholics were viewed with disgust and would certainly spend eternity with the devil in hell. They would be better served on earth by claiming they were Baptists.

My mother was in the choir when the Pope visited Detroit several years ago. It was a signal honor for her to be selected to sing for His Holiness. The entire ceremony was on television and we kids watched it for a while before switching to some sporting event. It was one of my sisters who apparently overcome with guilt told my mother that we had watched only half the ceremony. That was a mistake. A really big mistake. I mean telling her. This is a case of honesty carried to the extreme. She would have preferred to hear that we had torched the school.

We wore medals of saints, or scapulars, around our necks. Prayers were said before and after every meal. We knelt by our beds and said prayers every night. It was customary to conclude by asking the Lord to remember our loved ones—"God, please bless my mom and dad, brothers and sisters, grandparents and friends. Lord, I have a special favor. Are you listening? Please make me very rich and famous some day so my parents will be proud of me, but mostly Lord so those girls in my class who ignore me and won't go out with me will live to regret it. Amen." ◆

3

THE NEIGHBORHOOD

"Nothing makes you more tolerant of a neighbor's party than being there."

Franklin P. Jones

During my 63 years I have lived in 11 homes, from Seattle and Los Angeles to Dallas, Cleveland and Knoxville, but for fond memories and lasting friendships none compares with the little bungalow where I was raised on Kendal Street. It was then, and remains today, a middle-class, blue-collar neighborhood with well maintained frame homes, single car garages and manicured lawns. It was a stable neighborhood. People bought and stayed. Mothers remained at home to raise and discipline the children. They wore the apron, fixed the meals, cleaned the house and did the shopping at the corner grocery store.

Dads left early in the morning with lunch buckets in hand and returned for dinner in the evening, read the paper, and listened to a radio show or two before going off to bed. Growing up I knew only one person in the neighborhood who was divorced. Marriage was a vow not to be broken at almost any cost. (An aunt, a kind, beautiful woman, married a divorced businessman and was disowned by her father, my grandfather. In those days it was a scandal, an embarrassment. She was living in sin.)

Kids played in the street. Sometimes it was just playing catch or a crazy game like *One Step Off The Mudgutter*, or *Kick The Can*. There were some 40 kids in the 28 houses on our block so there was always some activity in the neighborhood. During the long summer evenings we played outside until the street lights came on. That was the signal to get into the house, clean up and get ready for bed.

It was a safe neighborhood. There was very little crime. House and car doors were rarely locked. I never had a house key during the 20 years I lived on Kendal. In every neighborhood, however, there are times when the serenity is broken and one is faced with the reality of a brutal crime. On our block it happened one summer evening just a few doors from home. The man of the house grabbed a butcher knife during a bitter argument with his mother-in-law and stabbed her to death. He ran from the scene but was captured, tried and sentenced to life in prison.

Another neighbor was executed. In fact, he was the only U.S. soldier executed during World War II. His name was Eddie Slovik and he lived six houses away. He was executed by firing squad in France on Jan. 31, 1945, after General Eisenhower personally ordered the execution during the closing days of World War II to deter other potential deserters. Of 21,049 U.S. deserters in the war, just 49 faced the death sentence, but only Slovik paid the ultimate price. In fact, Slovik, 24, was the only American soldier executed for desertion since the Civil War. The execution was the subject of a movie and book, *The Execution of Private Slovik*.

The neighborhood was made up exclusively of individuals of European descent. No Blacks, Hispanics or Orientals. We had Armenians, Italians, Polish, English and German, but we never thought of anyone in terms or their nationality.

Ann and Sark Hashoian, Armenians, had two children, Ralph and Joanie, and they were our next door neighbors. Mr. Hashoian owned a dry cleaning establishment on Chase Road. Ralph later became the art teacher at Edsel Ford High School. Growing up, Joanie was my sister Patty's best friend. They were terrific neighbors, one of the few in the area who had a dog. He was beautiful. His name was Blitz.

Then there was George Matesa and his two children, Larry and Caroline. Mr. Matesa worked at the Ford Rouge Plant I didn't know Caroline well, she was quite a bit older, but I will never forget Larry. He is one of those colorful people who you know will succeed in life and who seems to march to a different drummer. As a young kid he made a crystal radio, built complex model airplanes and constructed a homemade camera that worked quite well. At one time he was a stockbroker who the late J. P. McCarthy of WJR radio would call for an interview when the market was acting up. In fact, I bought my first shares of stock through him. It was Fruehauf Trailer which I sold at a modest profit when I bought an engagement ring. When he moved away, he cut down the cherry tree in the back yard and from it made a coffee table, something he could take with him as a remembrance of his boyhood home. He stood up for me at my confirmation.

The house was one that had been there long before the area was developed and so was older and different with a large front porch and no garage.

The photograph taken by Larry Matesa with his homemade box camera. The Matesa home is on the right. In the photo are neighbor Grant Huckabone and sisters Glenda (center) and Patty.

Buck and Martha Tomjak lived in a very neat home that had a floor plan identical to ours, except that we had a toilet on the main floor. They had one son, Ronnie, whose nickname was Dimble, and a niece and nephew from Seattle who lived with them for a few years. Ronnie's story is sad. In 1954 when he was just 20 years old he was diagnosed with leukemia. He lived only a few months. The Tomjaks had lost their only child. His girlfriend was Dorothy McCallion, my wife's best friend growing up.

I went to visit Ronnie in the hospital and will never forget the experience. It was evening. The sun was setting and the room was growing dark.

He was by himself in a large room with a high ceiling. Ronnie was in bed and he looked awful. He had a yellow cast. I didn't want to be there. I felt so fortunate when my visit was over and I walked out the door. For years afterward when I was at mass and we were asked to pray for the sick and deceased of the parish, he was the only one for whom I prayed. He was the only person I was close to who had died.

Ronald James Tomjak
Born, November 8, 1934
Died, June 1, 1955

Dewey and Virginia Lake had one son, Douglas. Dewey was a big man in the Masons. Virginia was subject to epileptic seizures which then was not something that could be easily controlled.

When I was five or six and Doug was eight or nine, he took me for a walk. It wasn't just a walk around the block. He took my hand and we walked to Oakman Boulevard, about a mile away. Before long, Doug arrived back home — alone. The kid just left me there. A kind lady saw me sitting on the median crying and knew I wasn't from the neighborhood. She took me home.

The McBrooms moved to the neighborhood from the South. They had two sons, Louis and Marvin. As a kid of about 10, I made a smart alec remark to Mr. McBroom one evening. He called my father. When I got home my father summoned me upstairs where he was doing some work on a bedroom window. He told me about the call from Mr. McBroom and asked for an explanation. I don't remember what I said, but I do recall that he casually, without any anger, whacked me on my hind end a few times and sent me to bed. I don't know why I remember this rather insignificant incident, but perhaps it is because my father didn't spank us often, and never when he wasn't angry.

I was in the McBroom home one afternoon when I spotted Marvin's trumpet on his bedroom dresser. I thought I'd give it a toot. As soon as my lips touched that mouthpiece and a short sound like a fart came out the other end, Marvin whipped around with eyes open wide, teeth clinched, face turning crimson. He started wailing on me. At first

I thought he was offended by the fictious fart, but it soon became clear that it was my bacteria-laden lips on his pristine trumpet that caused the kid to go berserk. I didn't know he was a clean freak. They eventually moved back South.

The prettiest girl on the block lived next door to the McBrooms. It was Marlene Lundgren, a beautiful blond. She had a brother, Leonard, who was good friends with my brother, Jack. Helmer, their father, had a Twin Pines wholesale milk route. I would help him occasionally on Saturday. He usually paid me $2 for about seven hours work. It was Helmer's relative who owned Lundgren's Ice Cream Parlor on Ford Road.

The Parkansky's lived next to the Lundgrens. They had six children, the second youngest of which was Bobby, my brother Tom's friend. Their house, like the Matesa's, was older than most others in the area and was there long before the area was developed. Mr. Parkansky worked for Ford Motor Company.

Mrs. Parkansky and I were sitting on her porch one morning. I was about 14 years old. Eddie, a young man I had known as an altar boy a few years earlier, came walking past the house. He had recently been ordained a Catholic priest and was wearing a collar. When he looked up at me on the porch, I said, "Hi Eddie. How ya doin?"

Suddenly there was Mrs. Parkansky's sharp elbow in my side as she smiled and said, "Good morning, Father." When he was out of ear shot, she turned to me, "Where in the world did you learn to call a priest by his first name? You should know better." At that she got up from her chair and went in the house. I think she was most upset because the good father might have the mistaken impression that the ill-mannered kid was one of hers. I reported the misdeed at my next confession even though I think it was just a venial sin.

We had a one-car garage like most of our neighbors, and like them we did not have a car until after the war. Our garage remained empty until 1946 when I was 11 years old and my dad came home with a brand new Pontiac. It was a blue two-door with manual transmission. Until then we really didn't need a car. My dad would walk about a mile early every morning to catch the streetcar on Warren Avenue and take it to work.

William Ford elementary school was only two blocks away. Tomkow's grocery store was even closer. There were no supermarkets. The Tomkows would sell groceries on credit, a bill we would settle every payday in cash. My parents have never owned a credit card and in those days didn't know about checks. Frank's Show Bar, with dancing and entertainment, was a block away on Chase Road. Also on Chase was the Apollo Cleaners and Dyers and the Mac and Dixie Barber Shop. The Dearborn Pizzeria opened on Chase about 1950.

The Scenic Gardens, a neighborhood bar on Ford Road, was an easy walk. On one side of the Scenic was a bakery and on the other side was the Alden Theater, one of three movie houses within walking distance. The Alden was the least expensive at 12 cents for a double feature and on a week day a piece of dinnerware came with the price of admission. During the war, admission was free from time to time in exchange for 20 tin cans that would be used for the war effort.

The Carmen Theater was on Schaefer Road. It was the most expensive of the three at 20 cents. It was a beautiful theater with a spiral staircase in the lobby leading to the refreshment counter. It also had a unique feature, love seats. These were seats for two scattered throughout the theater. The Midway Theater also was on Schaefer Road, but much closer to Michigan Avenue. Cost was 14 cents. I saw my first movie there. It was, *They Died With Their Boots On*, the story of the massacre of General George Armstrong Custer of Monroe, Michigan, and his troops at Little Big Horn. My good friend Larry Kliemann lived closest to the Midway so it was the one he and his brother Karl frequented. Larry claims that when they left home for the show, Karl would keep his eyes closed so they could find their seats in the dark when they got there.

The movie theaters in downtown Detroit were magnificent. Growing up I saw just one movie there. At my mother's insistence, my father took Jack and me to the Fox Theater to see *Going My Way*, a movie about two Catholic priests played by Barry Fitzgerald and Bing Crosby.

On Ford Road there was Lakes Printing; two drug stores, Sullivan's and Southern's; Lundgrens Ice Cream Parlor; and two restaurants, Brown's Fish and Chips and Taystee Barbecue. The son of the owner of Taystee's, Tony Coustas, is the owner of the Topper restaurant in West Dearborn. The City Hall was about one mile away and in the basement was the library. The big attraction there was the stereoscope, a device that allowed you to see two photos as one three dimensional picture, usually something like a herd of elephants in India.

Not far from City Hall was the Canteen. It was on the second floor of a building on a side street off Michigan Avenue and was open only on Saturday afternoon and evening. It was the predecessor to the Civic Center. There was a radio, ping pong tables, a pool table, a record player and a kitchen. The kitchen had the world's best grilled cheese sandwiches. The Canteen was a great place to meet your lady friends.

Most important for my parents, a Catholic Church, St. Clements, was only four blocks away. Not much farther was St. Barbara's where one of the masses each Sunday was said in Polish. St. Alphonsus was about one mile away.

Now, if you needed public transportation, the Steadman and Coleman buses ran frequently to downtown East Dearborn locations and from there you could catch buses in every direction. And, if you were lucky and standing at a bus stop, you might just have Mayor Hubbard stop, lean out the window and offer you a lift. It happened to my mother and she talks about it to this day. One might have disagreed with his policies, but he was quite a politician.

If you could not walk there, or buses didn't take you there, then often what we needed was delivered to our home. Doctors made house calls, and milk, bread, butter, coffee, ice and coal were left at our door. In addition, there was the Watkins man who would come every month with such things as cough syrup and vanilla extract. Our life insurance man came by every month to collect payments. Even vacuum cleaners were sold door to door. And there was always the Sears catalogue. ◆

4

SCHOOL DAYS

"In the 1940s a survey listed the top seven discipline problems in public schools: talking, chewing gum, making noise, running in the halls, getting out of turn in line, wearing improper clothes and not putting paper in wastebaskets. A 1980s survey lists these top seven: drug abuse, alcohol abuse, pregnancy, suicide, rape, robbery, assault (arson, gang warfare and venereal disease were also-rans.)"

George F. Will

My first exposure to a formal education was when my brother Jack took me by the hand in September of 1940 and led me two blocks to William Ford elementary school. It was there I was to first encounter many lifelong friends, including Jerry Lynch, Noralie Scott (now Steele), Larry Kliemann and Gary Gates.

The two-story school at the corner of Chase and Ford Roads was named after the father of Henry Ford, founder of the Ford Motor Company. The William Ford farm was located just one-half mile from the school.

William Ford Elementary School in the early 1920s before Chase Road was paved.

Alice Leitzke, my kindergarten teacher, was a kind, compassionate and competent young woman with the patience of a saint. She was followed by Mrs. Strang, my first grade teacher, who was blessed with the same qualities. For the next several grades, the teachers lacked patience and were older and stricter. Most had their gray hair in a bun and wore long matronly dresses. Of course then I thought 35 was old. There were two male teachers: Mr. Fell taught gardening, and Mr. Fleming was the gym teacher.

Mr. Fell was a bit of a character. Not the least bit fashion conscious, he always wore his pants low on his hips with his cuffs dragging on the floor and his wrinkled shirt sagging loosely over his belt. Any student who ever had him for a class will remember one thing in particular about him, and that was his accuracy with a piece of chalk. He could be illustrating on the blackboard the proper technique for planting corn or maybe drawing a dreaded weed, and suddenly he would whirl and with the fluid motion of a Nolan Ryan toss his chalk at an unsuspecting oaf in the back of the room who was caught whispering to his neighbor.

About two months before school was to recess for the summer, Mr. Fell would begin his once-a-week classes on gardening. When school recessed those of us in the seventh grade would be required to put to practice what we had learned in the classroom. Behind the school were what we called "victory gardens." We would arrive at 8 a.m., pick up a hoe, rake and shovel and proceed to our little eight-foot-square plot of ground to plant and maintain a garden.

WILLIAM FORD CLASS PHOTO

Top Row: Roy Rizzo, Mary Gilmartin

Row 2: Roger Moore, Barbara Toth, Noralie Scott, Don Sparpana, Richard Nikowski, Elaine Fields

Row 3: Don Papp, Ford McCammon, Pat Styles, Jackie Denaro, Joyce Battistone, Joan Kroll

Row 4: Ray Beaupre, Jerine Vowell, Stella Dougher, Janice Smith, Jerry Lynch, Bob Bierman

Row 5: Eileen McKelvey, Olive Patterson, Russ Chiado, Gary Gates, Ron Bruellisauer, Frank DeGrazia

Row 6: Marlene Lundgren, Phyliss Cady, John Marks, Margaret Schultz, Dolores Theisen, Pauline Fortuna

Row 7: Leonard DeRoch, Ralph Springfield, John Path, Ruth Lansing, Lura Sullivan, Gail Moore

58-5   Wm. Ford School
Dearborn, Mich.
Teacher Mary Schwartor
Gr. 6B

Mr. Fell had his own peculiar way of grading his students. In addition to report cards, he let everyone in the world know what he thought of their gardening skills by the use of various colored stakes. Each plot was graded with a stake. Blue stakes were for the best gardens, then there were red, green and yellow stakes. Yellow stakes were relatively scarce, reserved only for the worst gardens, where weeds and vegetables commingled. My little plot of ground was never graced with anything but a yellow stake.

Mr. Fleming was the school disciplinarian and this was at a time when corporal punishment at home and school was encouraged. Misbehave in class and you were sent to Fleming's office for a little attitude adjustment. He would administer one to five whacks depending upon the nature and severity of the crime. I think his paddle was tested in a wind tunnel. In any case it was extremely aerodynamic, with rounded corners. It had holes like Swiss cheese so that it slipped smoothly through the air. You only hoped that word did not get to your parents about your misbehavior, or just as severe, but less sophisticated punishment would be administered. Girls were exempt from Fleming's form of punishment, but teachers had other ways of keeping the class under control. Being kept after school to write, "I will not chew gum in school" on the blackboard 100 times or being kept in from recess were common. Mrs. Smith, the librarian, had a bizarre form of punishment. Misbehave and you spent the period stuffed under her desk by her feet.

Our music teacher, appropriately enough, was Ms. Sharp. She was a pretty woman and younger than most of the other teachers. She always used a generous amount of perfume, the pleasant aroma of which wafted throughout her classroom. I enjoyed her class. It was a no brainer. No homework. Nothing to study. Just show up and sing. Now I would always show up and when I opened my mouth something would come out but it could only be classified as singing in the very broad sense of the word. I was not blessed with a good voice.

My mother and every one of her 12 brothers and sisters had beautiful voices. Her brother Babe never took a lesson, but if you could hum a tune, he could play it beautifully on the piano. My father had a good singing voice as well. I have two nephews, Paul Bruce and David Bierman, who are musically gifted. Paul, my sister Glenda's son, has written a host of musicals, including, *A Perfectly Normal Boy* which was well received when it was performed in New York. David Bierman, son of my brother Tom, wrote several songs for his musical group, The Junk Monkeys, and was the lead singer. He has several albums to his credit. My son Randy is an accomplished organist and has composed a tune or two. This is a good illustration of genetics skipping a generation.

At the beginning of the year Ms. Sharp would call us up to the front of the room, one at a time, and ask us to sing a few bars of a song while she accompanied on the piano. This would allow her to seat us in the appropriate section of the room. It was always a troublesome experience for me. She would start playing and I would start singing. She stopped and looked up at me. She started again at a lower key. She stopped again. She turned the page to another song. She started. She stopped.

Some first and second grade William Ford students pose for the camera with their Halloween costumes in 1942.

She looked up at me and said, "Take any seat in the back row."

My handwriting is not really outstanding, but it is better than most men primarily because at William Ford we had a teacher who specialized in penmanship. She would come to our room for an hour once a week and teach us proper handwriting. She made the letters seem real, "Now don't forget children, when you make the small *r* remember that it is like a little house and the top of the *r* must slope down to the right so the water will run off."

At lunch time I would usually walk home, but if I were staying for lunch, I brought it from home. Only those kids who had rich parents bought their lunch at the school cafeteria. After lunch, we would head for the playground for a game of kickball or softball, or the guys would just hang around while the girls played hopscotch or jump rope. Like most young people, we would find some poor kid to harass. John Path was the unlucky soul we picked on. John was a tall boy with glasses, the studious type you could picture with a pen protector in his pocket. I do not remember how or why it started, but few days went by when we would not chant, "John Path is a Com-U-Nist, John Path is a Com-U-Nist, John Path is a Com-U-Nist." John ignored us, but I'm sure he was hurt.

Sometimes we would have four-man teams and run relay races around the playground. I was the fastest kid in the class. No question about it. One day I was approached by a boy who said he knew someone in our class who could beat me. When he told me who it was I scoffed at the very idea. It was Lura Sullivan. A girl. He had to be joking. Her father owned Sullivan's drug store on Ford Road and Williamson. (Its now a liquor store) I walked over to Lura and challenged her to a race. I wanted to nip this rumor in the bud. She refused to race. I pleaded. She relented

We took our places at an imaginary line in the gravel and decided on the distance at halfway around the playground. Word had spread and everyone stopped what they were doing to watch. I did a few deep knee bends and jogged out a few yards just to loosen up as Lura stood there, hands on hips. On your mark. Get set. Go. And we were off. Let me tell you that girl could run. She beat me by several yards. How humiliating. Beaten soundly by a girl. I challenged her to a rematch. She declined, probably because she thought it wasn't very lady-like. I didn't persist.

In the sixth grade our teacher announced there was going to be a school-wide talent show and every student was invited to participate. My best friend was Jerry Lynch. His nick name was

"Jeeps" because there was a car dealer then whose name was Jerry Lynch and he sold Jeeps. Anyway, he and I got together after school to discuss what talent we could contribute to the show. Singing was absolutely out as was playing a musical instrument, although we gave brief consideration to playing the comb. We certainly didn't want to recite some silly poem. We couldn't dance. I could run pretty fast, but what good was that in a talent show. The bottom line was we had no talent.

Jerry Lynch (right) and I pause during a game of catch at his house on Kenilworth.

The next day, I came up with the idea of doing a tumbling act. We checked a book out of the library, practiced several stunts for a few weeks and went on to be the hit of the show, although some said the tap dance routine by Richard Nikowski would have won had we been on the Ted Mack Amateur Hour television show.

Some of the snappy dressers in the sixth grade class at William Ford. Front row, from left, Russell Chiado and me. Middle row: Roy Rizzo, Ford McCammon, Frank DeGrazia and Jerry Lynch. Back row: Johnny Marks and Leonard DeRoch.

During winter the school was open from 7 until 9 in the evening on Monday, Wednesday and Friday for "recreation." Recreation consisted of shooting baskets in the gym or playing table tennis in the hallway. Mr. Jacoby supervised the gym and Mr. Byrd the hallway. Mr. Jacoby also supervised basketball on Saturdays at Lowrey school from 9 a.m. until 3 p.m. He was always kind enough to take me in his car if I was at his house by 8:30 a.m. His son Mickey and neighbor Ralph Springfield would go as well. It was that early exposure to the game and the frequent practice that gave me the incentive to pursue the sport.

William Ford school went through the seventh grade, after which we were promoted to Maples Junior High if we lived north of Donald Street and to Woodworth Junior High if we lived south of Donald. A few classmates close to Schaefer Road went to Lowrey. Unfortunately, Donald Street was only four houses south of us so many of my friends, including Jerry Lynch, went to Woodworth while I went to Maples, which was about one-half mile away.

Maples opened in the fall of 1930 and was named after Fred Maples whose family had a home in the Schaefer/Rotunda Drive area. He was prominent in civic activities and served on the Fordson Board of Education before the city was renamed Dearborn. The school replaced a log elementary school built in 1837.

On my first day at Maples, I was seated in the back row of an algebra class taught by a Mr. Bloink. He was fat, balding and mean, not my kind of teacher. He told us the class was larger than he expected and therefore he did not have enough books to go around. We were then told to come to the front of the class and take a book from the table. I took my time getting there, and as luck would have it got there too late; all the books were gone.

"Hey you, you doing the slow walk. What's your name?" Bloink asked.

"Bierman, sir. Bob Bierman"

"I saw you," he said. "You strolling up here real slow so you wouldn't get a book. I'm going to keep my eye on you. I know your type. You didn't want a book, did you?"

He didn't expect an answer and I didn't offer one although he was right on target about my intentions. I got a book a week later, but ever since then algebra is way down on the list of my favorite subjects. For that matter so is trigonometry, geometry and long division. I agree with Fran Lebowitz who said: "In real life, I assure you, there is no such thing as algebra."

My Uncle Harry tells the story of when he was in a math class and the teacher posed this problem to a fellow student: "Take 9 from 17, what's the difference?" The student, not too swift with math, but quick on his feet, responded: "That's what I would like to know, what's the difference, who cares."

Until I got to Maples my exposure to swimming had been a little wading and very little swimming at Sea Shore Pool in West Dearborn. We had no pool at William Ford. Now, I had swimming for physical education. When we were told to jump in and swim several lengths of the pool, I had to scramble for a position along one side because I could barely swim one length There were no swimming instructions because most of the students had been at the school since Kindergarten and were taught to swim in the early grades.

There was something about swimming class I liked even less than being told to go a few laps, and that was the dress code, or lack thereof. All 50 of us stood against the wall shivering, buck naked, while the coach took attendance. We were told suits weren't allowed for sanitary reasons, but strangely enough, the girls wore suits. I have been told, and I believe, that school uniforms help reduce disciplinary problems and eliminate status associated with clothing. But let me tell you, even the toughest guy in school becomes an introvert and much less aggressive when he's flopping in the breeze with a bunch of other guys.

At Maples, my homeroom teacher was Sarah Paull. She also had a dance studio and directed a number of musical shows for the school. Soon after I arrived at the school she drafted me into a small dance group that performed in all of her shows and a few parades in Detroit. Dick Reppa danced with me and later opened his own successful dance studio. I was not a very good dancer then and am little better today.

The teacher that made the biggest impression on me at Maples was George Sarkozy. He was a tough, very colorful physical education teacher who also coached track and was my first real basketball coach. Here's how he was described in the school's 50th anniversary brochure in 1980: "Who can forget George Sarkozy and his (in) famous paddle whose 40 plus years as a teacher, coach and administrator have been synonymous with Maples' achievements?"

In the fall of 1950 I rejoined my friends from William Ford when Woodworth and Maples students entered Fordson High School. The school was built in the late 1920s and is one of the most beautiful high schools in the country. Sports and dating dominated my life in high school. I had met my future wife, June Hopka, when we were in the

Maples Dance Group

Among the student dancers who went over big with the audience at the Maples School spring festival was this group which presented the "Peasant Polka." The pupils presented an evening of music and dances for both parents and classmates. Pictured in peasant attire are (front row) Carolyn Suriano, Jacqueline Denaro, Leonora Ptucha. Back row: Bob Bierman, Noralie Scott and Richard Reppa. The Maples dancers, under the direction of Sarah Paull, have built a reputation in the course of the past few years.

eighth grade, she at Woodworth and I at Maples. So Fordson was the first time we attended school together.

Fordson High School

Fordson is the only school in the state, and maybe the nation, to win state championships in swimming and basketball in the same year. That year was 1953 and I was fortunate to be a member of the basketball team. In February of the previous season, I was brought up to the varsity from the junior varsity and started the next game against Owosso. I scored eight points and started every game for the rest of the season.

In the fall of 1953, Don Greenleaf moved to Fordson from Henry Ford Trade School and George Colovas came to Fordson from Edison. Both were outstanding basketball players and made

62

significant contributions to the success we enjoyed that year. I am confident that without them we would not have won the state championship, even with John McIntyre and Dick Skruch, two exceptional athletes. John was an all-state player who later coached basketball at Fordson and for whom the school gym is named.

While Colovas and Greenleaf were good for the team, their presence did not bode well for me. Both were better players so I was left to alternate at starting forward with Bob Bohn. During the season we lost to Grosse Pointe, Highland Park and Dearborn. In our second match-up with Highland Park, a perennial powerhouse, we beat them 58 to 49 in what the Detroit Times called "the most startling upset in local basketball history."

When we entered the state competition, Fordson was ranked eighth in the state, Highland Park second. In the regional competition we whipped Jackson 62 to 40 and then went on to beat Grand Rapids South 53-46 in the semi finals. On Saturday, March 21, we faced unbeaten Lansing Sexton in the finals at Michigan State University's Jenison Field House. Lansing Sexton was 13 - 0 and had previously knocked from the tournament our nemesis Highland Park, 55 to 53. We went on the floor that night big underdogs, but came out triumphant, whipping the favorites 53 to 47. There were 1,257 spectators.

12,570

1953 Champions

SWIMMING TEAM

Bottom Row—George Stajanovich, Andy Boguski, Tom Kwasney, Bill Black, Virgil Schaffer, Ken Gest, Wyman Jacobs, Dave Antishin

Second Row—Bob Kanasty (Mgr.), Carl Sczewski, Dave Smith, Don Bender, Howard Fillmore, Bill Butzlaff, John Mikealian, Richard Rowe, Don Rupprecht, Tom Carlyon, Don Haskins (Mgr.)

Top or Third Row—Jim Wilkenson, Tom Gilbert, Bill Born, George Poulos, Bob Dyer, Radford Whiteman, Harold Lindeman, Bob Sellinger, Pat Fairman, Frank Czarnecki, Jim Dimoff, Gus Stager (coach).

Missing from picture—Steve Fordell, Dave Pleznac, Bill Harp

BASKETBALL TEAM

Top Row—Don Sparpana, Richard Skruch, Mario Perri, Gerald Mattson, Bob Bierman, Joe Opimach, Jerry Callaway, Don Greenleaf

Bottom Row—George Colovas, Bob Bohn, John McIntyre, Jim VanderHull (coach), Terry Callaway

We were the toast of the town. After the game, we walked into a restaurant in East Lansing and were welcomed by huge applause. The Dearborn Chamber of Commerce had a testimonial dinner for us and the swim team at Mt. Olivet Church. In attendance were Mayor Hubbard; Chuck Davey, a Fordson graduate who fought Kid Gavilan for the welterweight championship of the world; and Buddy Parker, Detroit Lions coach. Later, we were honored at a school assembly and at the annual activities banquet. The Dearborn Council issued a resolution congratulating both teams for bringing honor to the city and school.

That spring I was co-captain of the school baseball team with Pat McEvoy. We were starters on the team in our sophomore year, Pat at third base and I as catcher. In our senior year we won the Border Cities League championship and were honored at a banquet given by Mr. Ballou, a local restaurateur whose son Dennis was a pitcher on the team.

I was a pretty good hitter, batted .300 in my senior year, but I had one fatal flaw as a catcher: My arm was so weak I rarely caught anyone stealing second base. My best bet, I told some of my teammates, was for me to chuck the ball at the runner between first and second and by so doing stun him enough so that he could be tagged. I'm

Fordson varsity baseball team, 1952.

reminded here of what professional ballplayer Alvin Dark once said: "Any pitcher who throws at a batter and deliberately tries to hit him is a Communist."

Deaborn's most beautiful women pose in our living room before the 1953 senior prom. From left: DeVere Kosko, Dorothy McCallion, Pinky Higgins, Patty Bierman, Jean Crebassa, June Hopka and Ima Boatwright.

Everything has changed so much since the early 50s when I was in high school. Here's how Tom Beal of the Arizona Daily Star makes the point. *"When I was a boy, computers were the size of refrigerators, and they were slower than baseball games. Calculators weighed 20 pounds and were called adding* machines because they couldn't do multiplication. In school, we had to count on our fingers and toes and figure larger sums with a pencil and paper. And we had to sharpen the pencil by hand. We memorized multiplication tables and did long division by trial and error." ◆

5

MAKING MONEY

"Money may be the husk of many things, but not the kernel. It brings you food, but not appetite; medicine, but not health; acquaintances, but not friends; servants, but not loyalty; days of joy, but not peace or happiness."

Henrik Ibsen

A llowance? When I was growing up I didn't know what an allowance was. If I needed money on a Saturday afternoon to go to the Alden show I would ask my mother for 17 cents — 12 cents for the show and a nickel for candy. She usually obliged. And she rarely disappointed me when I asked for a nickel for an ice cream cone.

By the time I was 13, I was earning my own spending money. My first job was delivering the Shopping News. The paper was delivered once a week to every house in a 14-block area. I earned $1 a week. I did that for a year and then moved to the big time — The Detroit News. I bought a route with 54 customers. (We always pronounced route like it rhymed with out. When I heard someone pronounce it like it rhymed with root, I knew they were not in the business.) All of my friends had a paper route. At the time there were three major daily newspapers in Detroit: The News, Free Press and Times. My friends and I delivered the News. Later, for about one year, I had a Free Press route in the morning and the News in the afternoon.

It was not unusual to make $8 to $10 a week. With a little thievery some made even more. Every Saturday morning we had to collect from our customers and pay our bill at the station that afternoon. We collected 30 cents for daily delivery and 45 cents for daily and Sunday. It seemed like my brother Jack was always coming up short when it was time to pay his bill. He would stand there pulling dollar bills and coins out of every shirt and pants pocket. Just when it appeared he would be short, he'd find one more crumpled bill in his back pocket. He was thrilled when he had a dollar or two left over.

It was important to be alert when we stood at the bench folding our papers. It was not uncommon to have a paper filched from your stack by some kid who would have one or two more customers than he reported and would thereby pocket the entire 45 cents.

It is almost 50 years ago that I started delivering papers and I can still remember most of my News customers when I drive through the old neighborhood. There is one house I will never forget. It was Christmas Eve. Snow was falling and it had already turned dark. I was cruising along on my bike pulling folded papers from my bag and pitching them on the porch. As I approached the house on my right I knew it was going to take an accurate backhand toss with skill that came only with years of experience.

The porch was small and the paper was heavy. I pulled one from my bag, stretched my arm across my chest and then with my arm fully extended let that paper fly. It went whistling through the air like a helicopter prop, over the porch railing, past the canvas-covered chair and right through the bay window, striking the Christmas tree and causing it to topple to the floor.

I guess with Christmas and all, I had not taken into account the additional adrenalin rush that comes with the season. But I did what most kids would do. I got off my bike and hid behind a tree.

Eventually I confessed to my misdeed and delivered the paper free for a few months to pay for the damage.

Larry Kliemann at 15

My friend Larry Kliemann once tossed a paper through the window of a storm door. He stopped for a moment on his bike. His conscience got the better of him and anyway the paper was right there by the broken glass and it was obvious who the culprit was. He slowly walked to the front porch ready to own up to his misdeed. When he got there, he spotted the competitive Detroit Times and suddenly his conscience left him. He took a quick look around and deftly replaced his Detroit News with the Times.

From time to time there would be a breaking story that would warrant special attention. EXTRA would be displayed in bold letters across the front page. I remember getting one such edition of the Free Press. It was August 1948. I guess it was the movies that made me do it, but I soon was pedaling down the street at 6:30 in the morning hollering, "Extra, Extra, read all about it." Mrs. George, who lived behind us on Kenilworth, apparently was awakened by the disturbance. She slipped on a bath robe, and from her front door asked me about this really big news. I stopped my bike in the street and pointing to the headline, I shouted, "Babe Ruth died!"

When she said, "Who?" I knew right away she was not a baseball fan. Again I shouted, "Babe Ruth died." While she was some distance from me, I could still see the puzzled, then angry look on her face as she suddenly turned, went back in the house and slammed the door. Her reaction was enough to convince me that Extras were for the movies.

There always seemed to be plenty of ways to make money. Cutting lawns and shoveling snow were two obvious ways. I also would help neighbor Helmer Lundgren on Saturdays with his Twin Pines wholesale milk route. Good friend Dennis Doran and I collected cardboard boxes from behind super markets. For several weeks we would leave after school in his father's '32 Ford and collect all the cardboard boxes we could find. We would crush and store them in his garage. When the garage was half full we sold out. For all that work, we each got $2.

We always had plenty of money at Christmas time, much of it from tips from our newspaper customers. Even more lucrative, however, was Christmas caroling. None of us could carry a tune, but that didn't matter as long as we knew a few verses of one or two carols. Three or four of us guys would get together in the evening a few days before Christmas and go from door to door singing carols. We would walk to the porch, ring the door bell and start singing. Soon the porch light would come on, the door would open and we would be handed some money. That was the signal to quit singing and leave. We would dash off to the next house.

Unfortunately, there were always some individuals in the neighborhood who didn't understand the program They would invite us in! Often there would be neighbors visiting and word would spread throughout the house for everyone to gather in the living room to hear the carolers. It was awful. Even easy tunes like *Jingle Bells* sounded sour in the close confines of the living room, but that didn't stop them from making requests or applauding when we finished. Never again did we darken the front porch of those homes at Christmas.

Sometimes it took a little imagination to make a few bucks. My brother Jack and his friend Leonard Lundgren, Helmer's son, devised a scheme that is talked about to this day. It is marvelously simple, yet makes one sit in awe at how the mind works. It was a few days before Memorial Day and both Jack and Leonard had a case of the shorts, which was not all that unusual for Jack who, despite having a paper route, never seemed to be able to make it profitable.

They sat in Loretta's Confectionery on Chase Road wondering where their next dime was coming from. If only they had saved some of that easy loot they made at Christmas. From that thought it was only a short leap to their plan. If money could be made singing carols at Christmas, why can't money be made singing patriotic songs around Memorial Day? Why not indeed? They rehearsed right there by singing a few bars of the *Marines Hymn* and *God Bless America*. They sang very softly, not only because they could not sing worth a lick, but because they were concerned that some snoop might pick up on their idea. Soon they were off to make their fortune.

Departing Loretta's they bumped into Jim Rooney. Now, Rooney had a good singing voice, but that was of little relevance, and they did not want to share their take three ways. But the idea was such a good one, and they were so proud of it, they couldn't resist telling him. Jim immediately wanted in. He had a bad case of the shorts too. Jack and Leonard agreed to let him in with one condition. He would have to hide in the bushes next to the porch and while they sang the *Marines Hymn*, he would imitate bombs bursting in air, machine guns firing and shells landing. Rooney went along with the scheme. The guy was always thinking. While he kept it to himself, he was already planning a house-to-house singalong for St. Patrick's Day.

Unfortunately, history does not record the results of their endeavor, and Jack, Jim and Leonard have sworn an oath of secrecy. We can conclude from their reluctance to share the results that it was an embarrassing flop, or maybe that it was so successful they do not want others out there giving them competition.

There were occasions when I had to work for nothing. My dad had a Sealtest milk route, and often on a Saturday I would be awakened at 5 a.m. to accompany him on his route. My earliest recollection is riding with him in a horse-drawn wagon on West Grand Boulevard in Detroit. The side streets in the area seemed so full of life, so exciting and vibrant. Kids playing on the sidewalks and in the streets, loud music coming from cars being washed, people sitting on porch steps or taking a walk, and lots of laughter. I still can see a large Black woman leaning out of a second story window and shouting to my father, "I need two quarts of sweet milk."

The horse's name was Doc. He knew every house on my father's route. He was a good horse in that respect, but he had a very troubling habit. My father would return from delivering milk to a customer only to find the horse and wagon nowhere in sight. Doc had had enough for one day and was on his way back to the barn.

The first time I went on the route I asked my father how to make Doc turn when we came to a corner. He said it was really very simple. All I had to do was holler, "turn right" or "turn left." At the next corner, after my father told me what direction to turn, I leaned out the opening at the front of the wagon and shouted, "Hey Doc, turn right." And sure enough the horse turned right. When I turned around, my father was doubled over with laughter. He was raising a naive city boy.

When I started playing baseball and basketball at Fordson I gave up my paper route and started working part time at Brown's Fish and Chips on Ford Road. I worked there most Fridays as a bus boy or would work the take-out counter wrapping the fish in newspapers. Then, Catholics were not allowed to eat meat on Fridays. For hours the take-out lines stretched from the back to the front of the restaurant.

When Ford Road was made into a divided four-lane highway, all the businesses on the north side of the road, including Brown's, were demolished. The business moved to Greenfield Road where it thrived for a few years, but eventually came on hard times and closed its doors for good in the mid-1990s.

One of my more enjoyable jobs and one that paid quite well was delivering flyers for Mayor Orville Hubbard when he was up for re-election. We would gather at his home early on a Saturday morning and be taken by one of his department heads to an area of the city where we would deliver election leaflets door to door. Less enjoyable was working at bowling alleys setting pins before there were automatic pin setters. Pay was usually ten cents a game and work was a bit hazardous with pins flying everywhere. One place on Schaefer south of Michigan provided cots for derelicts who were pushed into service when pin setters were needed.

After graduation from high school, several of my friends and I were hired to work in Detroit at the Ordinance Tank Automotive Center (OTAC) operating IBM-card-sorting machines and other

IBM equipment. In the meantime, my future wife, June Hopka, was hired by Ford Motor Company as a secretary for the manager of the Ford Rotunda. She used her influence to get me an interview a few weeks before my 18th birthday. I was too young to be hired then, but returned a month after my birthday and was hired. When I left OTAC the sergeant in charge told me I would be back. "They all return," he said. I retired from Ford 41 years later.

While June helped me get the job, she came up short on my salary. It was $260 a month. Three months later it was bumped to $290, but I wasn't complaining. For a young kid just out of high school it was a wonderful, glamourous job, and besides, every spring we were provided with a suit and every fall with a suit and top coat. They were dry cleaned for us every week.

This was a case of knowing the right person who helped me get a job. I remember what Joan Rivers said at a commencement exercise, "You're a college graduate now, so use your education. Remember: It's not who you know, it's whom."

I was a tour guide. Tour buses left for the huge Ford Rouge complex every half hour in the summer and every hour in the winter. Some 30 college students were hired as guides during the summer to handle the huge crowds. On some days there would be six or seven busloads leaving the

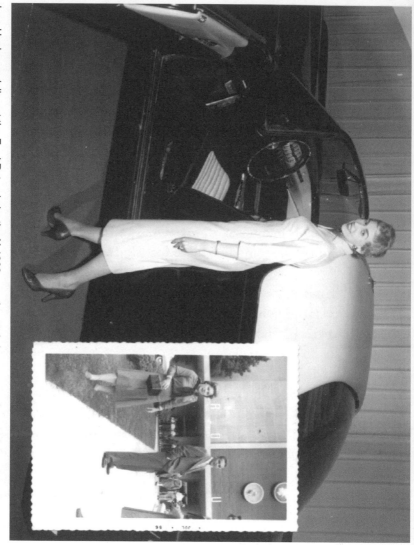

June Hopka modeling at the Ford Rotunda by the X-1000 experimental show car, and me in front of the Rotunda after taking a girl scout troupe on a tour of the Rouge complex.

Rotunda every half hour. We would take three, two-hour tours every day, consisting of the steel mill, stamping plant and final assembly plant. I still remember the spiel: *Looking out the bus window to your left you can see the Ford Rouge plant, the largest industrial complex in the world. It covers 1,200 acres or two square miles. There are 65,000 employees with a daily payroll of $1,250,000. The two parking lots now on your left and right and others in the plant can accommodate 22,000 cars. The Rouge is a city within a city. It has its own police force, fire department and hospital. The building coming up on your left is the engine plant. Pratt and Whitney aircraft engines were built there during the war. The tool and die building is to your right. Straight ahead is the steel operations building. It is one mile long and one-quarter mile wide at its widest point. Coming up on your right is the boat slip where we bring in raw materials: coal from West Virginia and Kentucky, limestone from Rogers City, Michigan, and iron ore from Minnesota. We burn 7,000 tons of coal a day, 200 tons of limestone and 3,500 tons of iron ore. And on your left is the final assembly plant. The building was first used to build Eagle sub chasers during the war....* The more experienced guides were eventually taken off the scheduled tours and assigned to "specials" which were school groups with their own bus and individuals who warranted special attention. The Rotunda was a fascinating show place and drew many celebrities, many of whom would take the Rouge tour.

While I met many interesting people during my tenure as a guide, there is one mysterious gentleman I remember in particular. After we had concluded the tour of the assembly plant and were waiting for the bus to return us to the Rotunda, this middle-age gentleman approached and thanked me for the tour. He then proceeded to tell me about an invention he was about to put on the market. It was a self-sharpening razor. The razor, he explained, had rollers along the length of the blade that would sharpen it as it was drawn across your face. It sounded feasible to me.

He gave me his business card and said he was looking for a young man like me who could take over his business in a few years when he planned to retire. He was not married and had no children to whom he could leave the business. "Come see me in Cleveland," he said when we parted.

As fate would have it, I was in Cleveland a few weeks later to work out with the Indians as the guest of Tom Okray's father who was the visiting team clubhouse manager. I called the "razor" man and arranged to meet him at his office. He was located on the second floor of a building in one of the poorer sections of town. A narrow, dark stairway led to his office. It was dirty and cluttered with papers, books, magazines and blueprints. We talked for a while about his razor and he showed me the blueprints. After about 45 minutes he bid me goodbye and said he would be in touch. He never called and I heard nothing more about his razor.

The Rotunda burned to the ground on November 9, 1962. I watched from the cafeteria in the Lincoln-Mercury building across the street, that at one time was the world headquarters for Ford and where Henry Ford, Henry Ford II and Harry Bennett once had their offices. When Henry Ford first occupied the building it was a male only environment. Later, when women were employed as secretaries, it became necessary to post a sign in the men's room which read: "Please adjust apparel before leaving." A reminder that women were now in the building and to zip up. That sign remained there well into the 1980s.

When I started college I chose to work evenings where I would walk the floor of the Rotunda answering questions and making sure rowdy kids behaved. After eight years of attending college part time and two years of service in the Army, I graduated from Wayne State University in 1963 and left the ranks of the tour guides to pursue a career in public relations. ◆

6
GAMBLING

"A man's gotta make at least one bet every day, else he could be walking around lucky and never know it."

Jimmy Jones
Hall of Fame horse trainer

When I reflect on my early school years, I am struck by how often we participated in minor forms of gambling. In elementary school the gambling was not for money, we didn't have any, but we did gamble for those things we prized.

Baseball cards and marbles are two examples. We seemed to have plenty of both. We played a game with baseball cards that involved from two to five or six kids. Standing in a circle, we would take turns fluttering the cards to the ground. The object was to flip your card on top of your opponent's in which case you won that card. It was not unusual to partially cover three or four cards with one toss.

There were several games of chance we played with marbles, the most popular of which was *odds or evens.* A player would pull a fist-full of marbles from his pocket. If his opponent correctly guessed the number odd or even, he won the marbles. He lost that number of marbles if he guessed wrong. Later, some kids, me included, learned to hide a marble between their thumb and index finger and would drop it into their palm or leave it out depending on which alternative would allow them to win.

While nothing of value changed hands, so to speak, there was even a bit of a gamble when boys stood at the urinals in school. You could be minding to your business at the urinal when some smart alec kid would walk in, and starting at one end, would move down the row of urinals calling out "Jap, German, Marine." This often necessitated moving in midstream to the Marine urinal before he reached you to avoid the humiliation of being labeled Jap or German.

My uncle Elmer lived in West Dearborn and visited us often. He had been bald ever since a friend in the Air Force persuaded him to shave his head. This, his friend had said, would result in thicker hair when it grew back. He was still bald five years later. One summer day he bet that brother Jack and I could not catch three of his pitches in a row. He pulled a quarter out of his pocket, flashed it close to our faces and set it on the pavement beside him. "That's yours. All ya gotta do is catch three easy tosses," he teased. He lied too.

I was first. I took my position in front of the garage door. Elmer stood on the driveway about 20 feet away fingering the ball while I adjusted my cap and took my stance. I caught the first toss with no trouble. Hardly needed a glove. Same with the second pitch. That quarter shining there on the pavement would soon be tucked in my pocket. I guess he didn't know how good I was. Bet he won't try this again. I stood there ready for that third pitch. Elmer hid any concern he might have had about losing a quarter. He took a slow, deliberate wind up, but when his arm came down it accelerated so quickly the ball left his hand like it was shot out of a cannon. I was still waiting in my stance when I heard something crash against the garage door. And then I saw the ball bounce halfway down the driveway. Elmer turned around. He didn't want me to see him laughing, but I could see his whole body shaking. "Next," he shouted.

Later, when we were old enough to make money on paper routes or by doing odd jobs, we played games for money. Pitching pennies against the Dearborn Pizzeria wall was common. We also played a form of odds or even with coins. This was another game at which it was easy to cheat. By holding the coin edgewise in your closed hands the coin could be dropped heads or tails making it possible to win every time if your opponent showed his coin first.

We also wagered on games of skill. My brother Jack and I had a ping pong table in our basement and with a lot of practice became quite proficient. After mass every Sunday we would invite our friends over for a tournament. Everyone would throw in a dollar, winner take all. If I didn't win, Jack did. We rarely lost. Eventually we had to start giving points and when we continued to win, they refused to get in the tournament unless we played left-handed. We did and still won most of the time.

It is hard to believe that one can win too much money gambling, but it happened to me. My friend Gary Gates challenged me to a game of horseshoes for $1 a game. I accepted and we set up the stakes next to a swing set on the William Ford school playground. I won the first three games.

On the next game we went double or nothing. I won again and was up $6. We went double or nothing for the next three games. I won them all and was now winning $48. It was double or nothing again. I won. He owed me $96.

I realized at this point that I would never collect $96 and that he would look on the debt as so ridiculous as to be non-payable. My strategy was to start losing. Unfortunately, it was not long before it became obvious to Gary that I was not putting forth my best effort, particularly when I put a ringer around the swing set support pole. He decided it was in his best interest not to win either. In fact, it would suit him better if he could just lose a few more bucks. So there we were, wildly pitching horseshoes that were landing yards from the stake. The charade ended when on a back swing I conked him on the noggin as he was bending over behind me to pick up a shoe. He bled. He quit. He never paid.

As we grew older we played poker in our basement and gambled a lot at the Scenic Gardens, the neighborhood bar that was owned by the father of classmate Pat McEvoy. The bartender was Jimmy Gilland, who later became the stepfather to my good friend, Jerry Lynch, after Jerry's father passed away. The bar, we sometimes called it the beer garden, had a bowling machine, bumper pool, and shuffleboard, games where one's skill could be tested and a wager placed.

Jerry Lynch and Chas, two regulars, were particularly skilled at bumper pool and over time had difficulty getting anyone to play them for money. No problem. They would take their skills on the road where they could fleece some naive rube. It was a wintery Sunday afternoon when we left for a bar in Wyandotte. I went along for the ride. Before long, two unsuspecting suckers had been enticed into a friendly game. The size of the wager kept increasing over time and after about two hours we grabbed our coats and walked out the back door. Lint was the only thing left in their pockets. ◆

7

ALTAR BOYS

Coming to the pulpit, the priest apologized for the Band-Aid on his face. "This morning while I was shaving, I was thinking about my sermon and cut my face," he explained. After mass, he found a little note tucked under his windshield wiper. "Next week while you're shaving," it suggested, "why don't you think about your face and cut your sermon?"

F ather Oakley was the pastor at St. Clements Catholic church when a number of my friends and I became altar boys. The good Father was a rather large man with a round, red face, white hair and a protruding belly. While he looked the jovial type, he was not. I seldom saw him laugh or smile.

It was said that he did not lack a sense of humor, but rarely was in a mood to be amused.

Father Oakley was appointed to St. Clements parish in 1939. He was born in Cork, Ireland, in 1890 and was ordained in 1914 at All Hallows College in Dublin.

As a chaplain in France during World War I, he was hit with mustard gas, damaging his vocal cords and leaving him with a deep, guttural voice that was often difficult to understand. It was that vocal impairment that later led to my premature departure from the ranks of the altar boys.

Father Oakley

Most of the time I enjoyed being an altar boy. In addition to assisting Father at mass, our other tasks included sweeping rice from the steps of church following a wedding, and replacing the burned out vigil lights. This latter job ended abruptly one Sunday morning when Gary Gates, in the process of changing the candles, had his loose-fitting surplice catch fire. It was quickly extinguished by a soldier in uniform home on leave, but thereafter the job was undertaken by adults.

I particularly looked forward to serving at funerals. It wasn't the service itself I relished, but the trip to the cemetery afterward. During the week it meant a half-day absence from school. Saturday and summer funerals were not a bit appealing.

There were six masses every Sunday -- 7:30 a.m., 8:30 a.m., 9:30 a.m., 10:45 a.m., noon and 1 p.m. Benediction was at the 10:45 mass. When we left mass, there was always a large crowd waiting at the door for the next mass. Every altar boy would serve at two consecutive masses. Before mass we would gather in the sacristy and decide among the more experienced who would ring the bells, hold the plate during Communion and perform other duties.

In those days the mass was in Latin, the priest faced the altar with his back to the congregation and was the only one to serve

93

communion. Meat was not consumed on Friday; women covered their heads in church with hats, babushkas or handkerchiefs, and no food or drink could be taken for several hours before receiving Communion. Waiting in line to go to Confession the Saturday before Easter Sunday could take up to two hours. Catechism was taught by the nuns on Saturday.

In addition to the regular collection, for which there were pencils and envelops in every pew, there was something called a "seat collection." Anyone occupying a seat was encouraged to pay a dime. There were indulgences one could pay for to help reduce the time one would spend in purgatory. The seat collection is a thing of the past, and very little mention is made today of indulgences, purgatory or limbo.

Weekday masses at St. Clements were at 7 a.m. I was serving alone at one of these masses when the incident occurred. I remember it vividly. About half way through the mass, Father Oakley, who was facing the altar, turned his head slightly in my direction and uttered something I could not understand. I genuflected and nervously approached him at the altar. Again, in a low, raspy voice he said what I understood to be, "Go get the *clost*." I had no idea what he wanted , but was afraid to ask again.

I left the altar and went to the sacristy desperate to find a cabinet or drawer marked *clost* or something similar. I searched frantically for a few minutes until suddenly I was struck on the side of the head and fell to the floor. Looking up I saw Father with a face several shades redder than normal standing over me shouting, "Don't ever leave me stranded on the altar again." Now, that I understood.

He need not have worried. I removed my cassock and surplice and left the church never to return again as an altar boy. ◆

8

DRINKING

From the tables at the poolroom
And on across Ford Road
To the dear old Scenic
That we love so well

There the boys are all assembled
With their glasses raised on high
And the rest of this old world
Can go to hell.

Gentleman Jerry off on a spree
Filled to the brim with whiskey
Lord have mercy on such as he
Strohs, Strohs, Strohs.

Words by Tommy Bruce
Sung to the Wiffenpoof Song

I was surprised one evening when Jim Rooney walked in the back door and grabbed a seat at the kitchen table. He had done this many times, but I didn't expect to see him that evening because I thought he was on his way to Ft. Knox. Johnson Pollock, Jim Steele, Morris Beernaert and Tom Okray had volunteered for the draft and were on their way to basic training. Jim was a tall, lanky lad who played on the St. Alphonsus basketball team. His father was a big union official at the Ford Rouge complex.

"What happened? I thought you left for basic training with the other guys."

It took him a while to answer. Finally, he turned to me and explained.

"Remember the night we got caught by the cops drinking beer in the Dearborn Pizzeria parking lot?"

I nodded.

"Well, that's on my record and the Army won't take me until its cleared, which will be in a few days. In the meantime, everyone else is gone. I'll never catch up with them."

I remember the parking lot incident well. It was a Friday evening and we were out of beer. We were under age, including Jim, but he looked the oldest and had a car, the Blue Goose. He was the least likely to be asked for proof.

We watched from nearby as he went into a beer store on Chase Road. Before long he emerged carrying a case of Strohs. We jumped into his car, there were six of us, and drove to the Dearborn Pizzeria parking lot. A poor decision it was.

The guys relaxing in the living room on Christmas leave (from left) Dennis Doran, Dennis Ballou, Jerry Lynch and brother Jack.

Jerry Lynch when he was stationed at the naval base in Pensacola, Florida.

It had to be less than 15 minutes, we were just starting our second beer, when all hell broke loose. I never experienced anything like it. Four police cars with lights flashing and sirens blaring came at us from all directions. We were stunned. They couldn't have responded with more force or with more precision if they were about to nail Jack the Ripper.

Instinctively, we reached down and tried to stuff our beer under the seats. It was futile. When the cops ordered us out of the car, beer flowed out with us onto the pavement. They took our names and released all of us but Jim. He was taken to the station and booked. The beer store was ordered closed for a week for selling to minors. Jim's record was eventually cleared, but he never did catch up with his buddies in the service.

(Jim and his wife Betty have lived in upstate New York since his graduation from Wayne State University in 1960. He was employed by IBM for 34 years as an engineering manager before taking early retirement. He is now working on his PH.D in Computer Engineering.)

Getting beer on a Saturday night usually was not a problem. We would put on a suit and crash a wedding reception. We had our choice of four halls — three on Oakman near Michigan and the Knights of Columbus hall on Michigan. We were rarely questioned.

Consuming beer unrestricted and at no cost often led to over indulgence. On one such occasion Larry Kliemann and I had crashed a wedding reception at the Knights of Columbus hall. By 11 p.m. Larry was drunk. As I was helping him out of the hall, he slipped from my grasp, fell backward against the door of the ladies room and ended up prone in a stall occupied by our friend June Hewitt. I pulled him out by his feet and took him home.

The gang on Kendal street propose a toast at the wedding shower for Jim Rooney and Betty Danowski. From the left are Tom Bruce, Jack Bierman, Dennis Ballou, Jerry Lynch and Jim Steele.

The next morning I went to his house and was invited in by his mother. Larry was sitting at the kitchen table with bandages over his eyes. He explained that he had recently purchased a pair of contact lenses, they were a relatively new product at the time, and in his drunken stupor had forgotten to remove them when he went to bed. He awoke the next morning and couldn't open his eyes. He was taken to the emergency room to have the contacts removed.

There was a barber shop on Chase Road across from William Ford school. It was owned and operated by Mac and Dixie, a husband and wife barbering team. They were outstanding barbers and did a great business. After work they were known to sit in the barber chairs and have a nip or two. One night they staggered from the shop with a load on. Several of us were assembled on the lawn at the school. Mac shouted at us. Would one of us drive he and his wife home. He was in no condition to drive.

Two of us volunteered. He gave us the keys, he and Dixie collapsed into the back seat and commenced to doze off. We were about 17 at the time and rarely had an opportunity to drive a car without our parents' close supervision. We drove all over the city that evening. The two bodies in the back seat didn't stir. After two hours we were getting low on gas so we parked the car in front of Mac's house, threw the keys on the front seat and left our passengers there to sleep it off.

That same barbershop was the scene of another drinking episode by a different barber who had bought the business. I went in for a haircut one afternoon the day before I was to make a trip with Larry Kliemann to see relatives in Illinois. When I entered the shop there was no one to be seen. I sat down and waited. Before long the barber emerged from the rest room.

"Have a seat young man. Have a seat," he said. "I only stepped away for a minute to answer nature's call. Ya know, when ya gotta go ya gotta go," he said with a laugh.

By this time he had me pretty well wrapped up in the chair. The guy talked non-stop. Relief from his constant chatter came only when he would excuse himself and duck into the rest room. So what if the guy's a jerk who likes to talk a lot. That can be said about a lot of barbers. That doesn't mean I can't get a good haircut, I rationalized.

Jimmy Gilland, the Scenic Gardens bartender, suddenly walked in the door, exchanged greetings and grabbed a chair. It was about this time my loquacious barber, who seemed to have a serious case of the runs, began to slur his words a bit and just the slightest odor of alcohol could be detected on his breath. Jimmy's ears perked up and he was now peering over the top of his Police Gazette. He had heard guys talk like that many times while he exercised his craft at the Scenic. The guy was drunk. Poor Bobby Bierman was trapped, but he was going to get the hell out of there.

"Excuse me," he said as he stood up and set the Police Gazette down. "I'm running late for a dentist appointment. I'll come back later," he said as he bolted for the door. I don't remember exactly what he said, but I know it was a lie.

When I got home my mother looked up from the stove as I walked in the back door. She gave me a double take before she screamed, "What happened to your hair?" After I looked in the mirror, I rushed to another barber, on Ford Road, hoping he could repair the damage. He helped a little.

One does things under the influence of alcohol that would never get the least consideration in the cold light of day. The Scenic Gardens was the sight of many wagers. After a few beers there was always a challenge of some sort on the table. The money would be put up and we would usually step outside for maybe a hundred yard dash by two guys half in the bag. For the endurance runners there would be bets on around-the-block races.

On one occasion Louie Zuzack challenged Jack Ewing to a race of one block. Before the bets were on the table, Tommy Bruce called Ewing to one side and offered to share his winnings with Ewing if he would agree to throw the race. Ewing nodded his approval. The fix was in. Bruce put a bundle on Zuzack. The bar emptied to watch the race. The smile on Bruce's face quickly faded when the race started and Ewing took off like a scalded dog. He led the entire race and won handily. Afterward, Ewing explained that he was just too competitive to not do his best. He could not stand to lose. It was an attitude that Bruce felt should have been shared just a bit earlier.

Ray Biedke, a muscular construction worker, and Ernie Christensen, the sixtyish part owner of the Scenic in later years, participated in the longest foot race. It was from Warren Avenue to Ford Road, about one mile. I don't remember who won, but they were both walking and gasping for air when they reached Ford Road.

My brother Jack often raced and usually won. Like many good horses though, he lost one race when he threw a shoe, a loafer. This caused him to lose his balance and he caromed into a brick wall face first.

The bar had more than its share of characters. There was Steve, Louie Zuzack's landlord, who lived on the opposite side of Ford Road from the bar. Ford Road was a busy street, but that didn't mean a thing to Steve. When he was ready to leave, he walked out the front door, across the sidewalk, down the curb and straight across the street without stopping or looking each way. Inside the bar, everyone went quiet. We could hear tires screeching and horns blowing, but Steve usually made it across without incident.

Then there was Johnny, who wasn't playing with a full deck. He could not hold his liquor and was limited to three drinks per visit. Often, when he was finished with his allotted amount, he would pay and walk out the back door. A few minutes later he would return through the front door, perhaps this time with a hat on, hoping he had tricked the bartender.

One night my brother Jack left the Scenic only to find that his car had been stolen. He returned the next afternoon and his car was parked exactly where it had been left. That couldn't be. He knew it had not been there the previous night. Later he learned that one of the bar patrons took Jack's car by mistake thinking it was his own and drove it home. The next morning the culprit's wife woke him up and asked, "Where in the hell did you get that blue car?" He looked out the window and scratched his aching head. His wife had asked a very good question. As it turned out, his key fit both cars, but amazingly, his car was automatic and Jack's was manual.

Most bars did not do much business on Sundays because it was against the law to serve liquor. At the Scenic, business on Sunday was like any other day. Care was taken not to be too cavalier about flouting the law, but it was easy to get liquor if you were a regular. You only had to keep an eye on the light above the cash register. If it was on, you could order, but if it was off that meant there

June and me in 1955 at KAS-SEE's in Toledo

was a stranger in the bar and no liquor should be ordered and shot glasses should be removed from the bar.

The drinking age in Ohio was 18 so we would often take our dates to Toledo where we could drink legally and enjoy a floor show. We frequented a place there called Ka-see's Theatre Nite Club... "Known From Coast To Coast." They had beautiful women selling cigarettes and a photographer who would take a picture of you and your date for a fee. On our first visit there they had an unusual female review. The women were beautiful and well endowed. It was only at the end of the show that it was revealed the gorgeous women were actually men and the male master of ceremonies was actually a woman. We were shocked. It was our first exposure to gays.

In the summer we would drink, often with our dates, at one of the Dearborn parks. We had house parties in the winter and there were bars in Detroit that served underage patrons. Drinking rarely resulted in a problem. However, I know of one school friend who started stealing from her father's liquor cabinet at the age of 12 and by high school was a full-fledged alcoholic. I was not aware of her problem until years later even though she attended many of our parties. She is now a recovering alcoholic. ◆

9
KIDNAP CAPER

"You can fool some of the people some of the time and you can fool all the people some of the time, but you can't fool all the people all the time."

Abe Lincoln

Young kids with fertile minds, time on their hands and a willingness to carry out their wild ideas are the ingredients that can spell trouble, and did for the gang on Kendal Street one summer afternoon.

We were bored. We had played a little softball earlier in the day and now were in Loretta's

Confectionery sipping Cokes and ruminating about the lack of excitement in our lives. We were 17 years old, going into our senior year in high school, and life was passing us by.

There were four of us seated around the table. In addition to me, there was my brother Jack, Dennis Ballou and Larry Kliemann. Several thoughts for adding a little spark to our life were laid on the table and dismissed. Eventually there was just the tiniest germ of an idea that surfaced and appeared to have some promise. The more we kicked it around, the more excited we became, and within just a few minutes we had fine-tuned an outlandish, bizarre plan. We were going to stage a kidnapping! This was not going to be just an old run-of-the-mill kidnapping. We were going to kidnap someone who was in on the caper, namely Larry Kliemann.

First we needed a car. Larry volunteered to get his father's. This is the same ingenious Larry Kliemann who got his father in trouble at the bank just a few weeks earlier when he went in to cash several rolls of dimes. The teller at Manufacturer's National Bank questioned Mr. Kliemann's honesty when he noticed that each roll was one dime short. Larry was the culprit. He was smart enough to know that one full roll would be missed but maybe not one dime from each roll.

Larry brought the car to Loretta's, we piled in and headed for West Dearborn. When we got to the outskirts of the business section, we turned down a side street off Michigan Avenue and pulled to the curb. We reviewed the plan one final time with Larry and watched as he left the car and headed back toward Michigan Avenue. His destination was the Cunningham's Drug store on the corner of Michigan and Monroe.

Larry moved quickly past the crowd waiting at the bus stop and entered the side door of the drug store. He went to the girl behind the soda counter. Fidgeting with his wallet and looking nervously over his shoulder, he asked the girl for change for the phone and would she please hurry. He had to make a very urgent phone call.

In the meantime, we turned the car around and began heading very slowly back to Michigan Avenue and the drug store.

Larry took the change and continuing to make furtive glances over his shoulder, walked nervously to the phone booth just inside the side door. He slipped a dime in the coin box as we pulled up in our car at the side entrance. Jack and Dennis stepped from the car, moved quickly past the crowd at the bus stop and into the store while I stepped to the back of the car and opened the trunk.

Jack and Dennis forced open the phone booth, grabbed Larry as he struggled, and dragged him screaming out the side door and past the crowd. They shoved him into the trunk, slammed it shut and jumped in the car as the crowd looked on in stunned silence. Larry's muffled cries for help could be heard as I stomped on the accelerator, leaving a patch of rubber on the pavement.

We laughed all the way back to East Dearborn where Larry was let out of the trunk. The plan was perfectly executed. We were so proud. That was all the excitement we needed for one day. But there was more to come, excitement we hadn't planned on.

Larry and I went to Anthony Park to watch a softball game. We were sitting in the bleachers laughing because a friend had just stolen third base only to find it already occupied by one of his teammates. I spotted my brother moving briskly toward us from the parking lot. I could tell by the look on his face, something was wrong.

"I've been looking all over town for you guys. You're in big trouble," he blurted when he reached the bleachers.

"Why? What's the problem?" Larry asked.

"Your dad's in jail," he said.

"What the hell did he do now?"

"The cops picked him up at your house and took him in for questioning. Someone at the

Cunningham's bus stop got the license number of your car and reported that it had been involved in a kidnapping. They traced it to your father. He is really pissed. You better get to the station and explain what happened," Jack said.

By this time Larry was jogging toward the car. He turned and shouted at me, "C'mon, Bob. You coming with me?"

"Noooo. I don't think so. I'll just go home with Jack. I've had enough excitement for one day."

◆

10

PLAY BALL

"The highlight of my baseball career came in Philadelphia's Connie Mack Stadium when I saw a fan fall out of the upper deck. When he got up and walked away the crowd booed."

Bob Uecker

I was playing left field in a baseball game against the inmates at the high security prison in Jackson, Michigan, and I misjudged a few long flies, let a grounder or two get past me and made a couple bad throws. All in all it was a pretty poor performance. But I took consolation in the fact that I was a catcher, not an outfielder. And I was a decent catcher — played in a few all-star games, captained my high school team and was not bad at the plate. Anyway, my brother-in-law, Tommy Bruce, was playing third base. Between innings he was standing at third when he said to the prisoners' third base coach, "You guys sure have a tough team." They were tough, and obviously had the advantage of playing every game at home. The burly coach looked at Tom and nodding toward me in left, said, "Lessen you get yoself a new lef fielder, every team you play is gonna be tough."

Sports were a very important part of my life growing up. At every opportunity I was playing baseball, softball or basketball, or some form of those games. There were father and son softball games, one of the few occasions I could spend leisure time with my father. Afterward, we would go out for ice cream at Gerties on Chase Road. I played a lot of organized ball, but I remember most fondly those spontaneous games where a bunch of guys got together in the neighborhood and went to the park to play. Sometimes we would pick sides and at other times we would have established teams.

We had a team on Kendal and there was also a team on Kenilworth, the street behind us. We would often play in the park on Chase Road next to the Dearborn Pizzeria It's the same park the fire department flooded every winter to form an ice rink. A big sign there now says "No Ball Playing." That doesn't include boccie ball which is played there often.

Not all of the players lived on Kendal or Kenilworth. Gary Gates, for example, lived on Middlesex but always played with Kendal. We had some great games and a lot of fun. Many years later Gary still remembered those games when in my copy of his best-selling book, *The Palace Guard*, he inscribed, "In fond and enduring memory of all the years, from the Kendal - Kenilworth days on."

Later we played games at Oakman School almost every Sunday during the summer. It was called the Bobby Oakman league, but it actually consisted of just two teams. We played for beer, the loser buying. We were playing one Sunday, I recall, when we started a game with just eight players and so had no one covering right field. An opponent crushed a pitch that carried deep to right, a sure home run. As luck would have it, Iggy, a regular at the Scenic Gardens bar, stepped in the right field gate, looked up and casually caught the ball in his bare hands. "Iggy's our right fielder," we quickly screamed as our opponents registered a strong protest.

If we didn't have enough players for a game, we would go to William Ford and play "strikeout." This we could play with one, two or three players on a team and all we needed was a bat and a well used tennis ball. It was simply a matter of hitting the tennis ball as it was being pitched against the school wall. We used a slightly worn tennis ball because it was easier to throw a curve. It proved to be an excellent introduction to the curve balls we would face when we eventually played competitive baseball.

I caught a few fast-pitch softball games and found it much more difficult than catching baseball. The softball got there quicker and a good pitcher could get it to move in every direction. Hitting the ball was even more difficult than catching it. My brother Jack once hit a line drive single over third base. It was a good hit off a fast ball that was breaking inside. Jack took a swing and hammered that ball — not with his bat, but with his forearm.

My good friend and great athlete, John McIntyre, not only was the basketball coach at Fordson, but also managed a softball team on which I played for a few years. John was the ultimate competitor in those days and had a temper to match. Before one night game, as was customary, he gathered his team to go over the lineup and other details. The umpire called John and told him to get his team on the field. John wasn't finished with his meeting, he told the umpire. The umpire persisted. John didn't move. The umpire removed his mask and walked half-way toward John. He was steaming.

"You're outta here." he said. "I'm throwing you out of the game."

"What the hell are you talking about. You can't throw me out of a game that hasn't even started yet," John logically countered. "You're not even officially in charge here yet."

"Yes I can and yes I am. I don't even want to see you in the stands as a spectator."

The umpire won. John has the distinction of being the only player in Dearborn history to be ejected from a game before it started.

As he left the field, he showed his disgust by kicking over the trash can.

A season or two later John was involved in another bizarre incident at Hemlock Park. It was a slow pitch softball game. John was playing short stop, his brother-in-law Rich Lopez was at second base, and the manager, Tom Bruce, was playing third base. A high pop up was hit toward second base.

"I got it," Lopez shouted.

"It's mine. I got it," McIntyre said as he drifted under the ball, bumped Lopez out of the way and caught the ball.

"What are you doing," Lopez screamed. "I called for the ball."

"So did I," John countered.

"Look where you caught the ball, right in front of my position. You idiot," Lopez said as the argument quickly turned to name-calling.

Finally in frustration, Lopez, standing nose to nose with McIntyre, spit out the worst of insults, "Your mother wears combat boots," he said.

With that, they dropped their gloves as if they were in a hockey game. Players from both benches were on their feet, as were the spectators. Tom Bruce left his position and moved quickly to separate the combatants.

"I refuse to play with that fool," Lopez said of McIntyre.

"I never want to be on the same field again with that idiot," McIntyre said of Lopez.

"Decide right now, Bruce. Who's it going to be, me or Lopez?"

A hush grew over the crowd as Bruce contemplated this very sensitive situation, one that required the wisdom of Solomon. Finally, he removed his hat, scratched his head and uttered those famous words: "Eenie, meenie, miney, moe, O, U, T, spells out you go," at which time he was pointing at McIntyre. "You're outta here, John," he said. ◆

11

THE RUNAWAYS

"The young always have the same problem -- how to rebel and conform at the same time. They have now solved this by defying their parents and copying one another."

Quentin Crisp

It was about midnight when from my upstairs bedroom I heard the phone ring in the dining room. My mother answered it and soon was opening the door to our bedroom. "Mrs. Gates is on the phone and she's very upset. She wants to know if you know where Gary is. He hasn't come home."

I propped myself up on my elbow and said, "He ran away." She looked at me. "He ran away," I said again. She stood in the doorway for a moment. She heard me and now she had to get back on the phone and tell Mrs. Gates, not a pleasant task under any circumstance but doubly difficult when dealing with Mrs. Gates. She was a strict school teacher with flaming red hair who was not the least bit fond of most of Gary's friends. "The Kendal Street gang" was her less-than-endearing description of us. Later she was heard to say, "The Bierman boys, they're the ones who encouraged Gary to run away and then they stayed home."

Earlier in the evening after shooting baskets at recreation, I walked into the lavatory at William Ford school. Standing by the wash basins having a serious discussion were Gary Gates, Larry Kliemann, Dennis Doran, Tom Okray and Jerry Lynch. All had skipped school that day to watch at Kliemann's house the 1951 National League championship game between the Brooklyn Dodgers and New York Giants. The game was settled in the ninth inning with a home run by Bobby Thompson. It was one exciting ball game, one worth skipping school to watch. But their truancy had been discovered by school officials, and parents would be notified in the morning. (This was no big deal for Larry Kliemann. He claims he once skipped school for

27 consecutive days and occasionally called in sick from the school's phone.) What to do? They would run away from home, that was the answer. "We're going to California," they lied. Actually they planned to go to Florida but hoped to put parents and police off their trail.

They went home to get what money and food they could. They returned with $7 in cash and several cans of soup and beans. It was about 9 p.m. when they bid us farewell. Russ Chiado and Lloyd McDonough drove them to the corner of Telegraph and Ford Road where they stuck out their thumbs and started the trip south. That evening they managed to make it to Toledo. The final ride was from a college student who invited the five to stay in his apartment for the night. The next morning he drove them to the outskirts of Toledo and wished them well.

By that evening they had made it to Columbus, Ohio. Sitting in a drug store that night they were asked by the manager if they wanted to make a few bucks by cleaning out the storeroom. They jumped at the opportunity and made enough money to stay in a hotel that evening. Two paid and three sneaked in the back door.

The next morning they decided it would be easier to catch a ride if they were to form two smaller teams. Larry and Gary volunteered to be a twosome.

They left the other three and made plans to meet again at the capitol building in Charleston, West Virginia. Gary and Larry managed to get to Nitro, West Virginia, that evening. Gary asked a couple he met on the street to put him up for the night. They did, but Larry continued on to Charleston because he expected his three mates to be waiting for him at the capitol. He arrived in Charleston late that night and slept in an unlocked car in a used car lot near the capitol. It was a cold and lonely night. He spent the entire next day walking around the capitol building in search of his fellow runaways. They were not to be found. He spent another night alone in the used car lot.

Gary arrived the next morning and together they spent the day waiting at the capitol for their friends to arrive. They didn't. So, it was another night in the car. It snowed. They made some money the next morning shoveling snow, but spent most of the day in the warmth of a hotel lobby. The sympathetic manager let them stay when they explained their parents were having car problems. The Greyhound bus terminal was their home that night.

They concluded that something had happened to their friends and they could no longer afford to wait for them in Charleston. As it turned out, the other three, after just a few days away from home, had decided that life on the road was a bit tougher than they had expected. They simply crossed the street and started hitching a ride home. For Gary and Larry, it was time to move on. The next morning they hitched a ride to Beckley, West Virginia. They had been without food for some time now and were getting desperate for a good meal. They needed money. Rolling a drunk was their first thought, but they dismissed that idea when they could find no bars and concluded West Virginia was a dry state.

An opportunity presented itself when they found themselves walking behind two elderly women, both with handbags. After several minutes, Larry garnered his courage and made a sudden dash for the startled ladies. He snatched a purse, made a sharp right turn, ran between two houses and suddenly found himself tumbling down a 40 foot embankment. He ran a short distance before opening the purse and removing $20. He discarded the purse. Gary, somewhat stunned by Larry's action, consoled the ladies, pretending he was not with that degenerate, no-account purse snatcher. He said he would have chased the thief, "but the lard ass, I mean fat boy, was pretty quick for his size."

They had a good meal and went to see a movie starring Rhonda Fleming. It was dark when they left the theater and decided they would head south that night to Bluefield, West Virginia. As they headed toward the outskirts of town, they decided to use the police station rest room to relieve themselves. Maybe subconsciously they wanted to be caught or perhaps it was to show their disdain for the "hick town" cops. In any case, they were arrested before they could reach for their zippers. The ladies, one a retired school teacher, had described Gary to a T, freckles, red hair, even though they were not sure he was in on the caper. Larry was described as a Negro youth.

They were taken to the victim's house where they were identified. She was a kindly old lady who would not press charges, but wanted her purse back because it contained her glasses. The police officer took the criminals to the embankment where the purse snatching occurred, handcuffed the two together and tossed them over the side. "Find that purse," he shouted. They did and it was returned with the little cash they had left. Gary and Larry were jailed for a few days until their parents came to retrieve them.

Upon his return to Dearborn, Larry quit school, worked for a year, joined the Army and served in Korea as a cook. He later got his high school diploma and retired from Ford Motor Company. It took him nearly 45 years, but he finally made it to Florida and now lives with his wife Joyce in Vero Beach. He calls it Paradise.

Gary returned to Fordson where he was an outstanding student. He graduated from Notre Dame, wrote for United Press International and eventually moved to New York where he now lives. He has written several books, including *The Palace Guard*, the best-selling, behind-the-scenes account of the Nixon Administration which he co-authored with Dan Rather. ◆

12
VACATIONS

"A tourist is a fellow who drives thousands of miles so he can be photographed standing in front of his car."

Emile Ganest

There we were, my good friend Larry Kliemann and I, leaning up against his car parked at the side of a two-lane highway next to an Iowa cornfield. It was a hot Sunday afternoon as we chucked stones at a nearby fence post waiting for a tow truck to haul us to the nearest town. We had left our home two days earlier heading for California in Larry's new 1956 pink and white Mercury convertible. Disaster was to strike many more times before we were safely home.

Larry and I had gone on many vacations together, traveling to such places as Saugatuk, Michigan; Toronto, Grand Bend and Montreal, Canada, and to my relatives in Moline, Illinois. Larry still bears a few scars from our Grand Bend trip where we made the mistake of roller skating at an outdoor rink after we had more than enough to drink. Sober, Larry is not too well coordinated. Drunk, he should never get on skates. He fell a dozen times and would have fallen more had it not been for the railings. When he was upright no one on the floor was safe. Bodies were falling everywhere. Finally, he was ordered to leave.

My most memorable vacation up to this time was when Larry was in the Army and I flew with Jim Steele and Jack Robinson to Miami. It was my first trip on an airplane. The flight was advertised in a small classified ad in the Detroit News. We flew out of Wayne County airport on a two-engine prop plane and refueled in Knoxville. Shortly after leaving there we ran into some very turbulent weather. The plane was bouncing and rocking constantly. Breakfasts consumed two hours before were now being deposited in paper bags.

It was in this environment that I noticed one of our two engines was no longer operating. We thought nothing of it, assuming naively that this was standard procedure. Finally we descended through the clouds and I could see the airport runway next to which was a fire truck with lights flashing. This sure didn't look like Miami. It wasn't. We were back in Knoxville. Repairs were made and several hours later we were on our way again to Miami.

The same plane was to take us home. It was seven hours late leaving Miami. As we were standing in line waiting to board, I overheard a man

Larry Kliemann strikes a familiar pose on our trip to California in 1957.

131

behind me say, "Mother, we're in the wrong line. Thank God. I could never let you get on that plane. It looks like it won't even get off the ground."

Back in Iowa, our tow truck finally arrived and towed the car with us inside to an auto repair garage a block from the only traffic light in town. It was Sunday and the shop was closed. Fortunately there was an emergency phone number on the door. We called and the owner of the shop left a family gathering to help us with our problem. Before long he had the car running again, that is it would run forward, but not in reverse. Reverse was an option we had learned to live without for the last several hundred miles. Since after breakfast, when we had to push the car away from the restaurant, we avoided situations where reverse would be necessary.

The mechanic did not have the skill or the equipment to fix transmissions and suggested we stop at a Mercury dealership in Lincoln, Nebraska. As we prepared to leave, he rubbed his hand over one of the front tires and asked, "How old is this car? It looks new."

"Why it is new. Bought it new just a few days ago. Has only 1,000 miles on it," Larry explained. "Why do you ask?"

"Your front tires are bald," the good man said. "You better get new tires when you're in Lincoln and get your wheels aligned while you're at it."

Early Monday morning we took the car to the Mercury dealership in Lincoln. The technicians there had us on the road again Wednesday morning and by evening we were approaching the Rockies. With two days lost in Lincoln, we decided to continue on into the mountains. As dusk gave way to darkness, we turned on the headlights. The bright lights illuminated the hairpin turns, switchbacks and steep grades. Before long we realized we had a problem. The lights would work only on high beam. Approaching traffic would signal us to lower our beams and when we wouldn't, couldn't, high beams were kept on us. This was not the time or place to be blinded by oncoming traffic. We pulled in for the night and continued to see stars even as we lay in our motel room.

Eventually we made it to California and caught up with our friend Dennis Doran in Torrance. One afternoon he drove us in Larry's car on a tour of Beverly Hills. On our return to his home, I expressed some concern about how close he was coming to the cars parked at the curb. "Don't worry. I drive like this to work every day, " he said. A few moments later we got a tad too close and hit a car, knocking off our mirror and scraping the entire right side of the car. "Sorry about that," was the curt apology that followed.

We left California the next day by the southern route. In West Texas we encountered a terrible rain storm. Unfortunately, it soon became as wet inside the car as it was outside. Rain literally poured in every crack. Top up or down would have made no difference. We and everything else inside the car were soaked.

Nothing of consequence happened during the balance of our trip. We left home in a beautiful, spanking new Mercury convertible. By the time we returned, we had replaced the transmission and tires, encountered a starting problem and had the wheels aligned. In addition, the headlights worked only on high beam, there was no right-hand mirror, the right side of the car was severely damaged and it leaked so bad umbrellas should have been offered as optional equipment. Thank God they don't build them like they used to.

In the summer of 1954, during my early years as a guide at the Ford Rotunda, Eugene Brusco dropped by and asked if I would like to join him, his cousin Gene Osso and Skip Rheault on a trip to New York City. A few days after I accepted his invitation, I met a girl from New York while conducting a tour of the Rouge and I told her of my plans to visit the city. She gave me her phone number and asked me to call. When we got to New York, we did all the things tourists do — Statue of

Liberty, Empire State Building and Radio City Music Hall. We also went to the famous Stork Club for a few drinks and dinner. When we left, the waiter noticed our tip, a miserly one in his judgement, and in typical New York fashion let his opinion of us be known to all within earshot. And the place was crowded, reminding me of what Yogi Berra once said, "Toots Shor's restaurant is so crowded nobody goes there anymore."

The next morning I called the girl I had met at the Rouge and made arrangements to meet her and three of her girl friends that evening in the lobby of a Manhattan movie theater. During dinner with the guys I excused myself and walked two blocks to the theater. I told the girls we were at dinner, but that I would be back in just a few minutes. When I returned to the restaurant, the guys had decided not to go to the show. My pleadings fell on deaf ears. We stood up those poor girls.

We did a lot of bar hopping and consumed a considerable amount of alcohol. Stepping outside one bar, Skip said he didn't feel well and looked a bit pale. A moment later he walked over to a trash can, lifted the lid and unloaded the contents of his stomach. He replaced the lid, wiped his mouth and joined us as we walked into another bar. He carried on as if he had done nothing more than blow his nose. What staying power. It was author and humorist Lewis Grizzard who said, "On a New York street you can get fined for spitting, but you can throw up for nothing."

On our return trip to Dearborn, we stopped overnight in a small Pennsylvania town where a county fair was being held. Inside one of the tents was a man in overalls standing by a chest-high table. I peeked over the shoulders of the onlookers and saw three half walnut shells, under one of which was a pea. He moved the shells around and would wager we couldn't pick the shell under which the pea was hidden. I couldn't believe it. Anyone with two eyes could follow the shell with the pea. I worked my way to the front and laid a dollar on the table. He lifted one shell to show me the pea and then started moving the shells as I concentrated on the one with the pea. Easy money. I pointed to the right shell. He lifted it, but there was no pea. How could that be. I bet again, and again. Lost and lost and left shaking my head at how my eyes could deceive me so. It was a cheap lesson — not everything is as it appears.

One summer day on our way to visit my relatives in Moline, Illinois, Larry and I stopped in Calumet City, at that time a wild Illinois town with open gambling and prostitution. It was the kind of town Gustave Flaubert had in mind when he said, "The man has missed something who has never left a brothel at sunrise feeling like throwing himself into the river out of pure disgust."

We went into a bar and had a few beers. When it came time to pay, Larry searched his pockets frantically for his money. Someone had picked his pocket, he claimed. The strange thing about it was that Larry still had his wallet so the thief would have had to remove it from Larry's pocket, take the money and replace the wallet. "What a thoughtful pickpocket," I said "He wanted your money, but knew how sad you'd be without that picture of your sweet girlfriend. What a guy. Now there's a pickpocket with class." Larry sticks by his story. ◆

13

FEAR OF FAILURE

*"Folks who call themselves 'Fillmorons' hail Millard
Fillmore as a man who perfected mediocrity, someone whose
sheer obscurity stands out like a beacon. Everything he
touched turned to lead. The preservation of Fillmore is a
way to give underachievers and little people someone to look
up to."*

Society for the Preservation and
Enhancement of Millard Fillmore

I was in a conversation with two friends many years
ago when one of them turned to me and said,
"It seems to me that you are very good at everything
you do." Before I could reply, my other friend
interjected, "Did it ever occur to you that Bob does
only those things at which he is very good." He
had a point. A strong fear of failure and a lack of

139

self confidence causes one to be very cautious about exploring the unknown.

Growing up was a very happy experience for me. My brothers, sisters and I have always been very close. We fought, argued and often belittled one another, but we always stuck together when it counted. Four of us were born within six years, which I suppose accounts in large measure for our closeness.

We lived in a modest, comfortable home in a middle-class neighborhood. I never really wanted for anything and I never felt I was any better or any worse than anyone else in my class at school or in the neighborhood. I was a normal kid, in a normal, healthy home environment, with normal friends and normal relationships, yet my self esteem was lacking.

It is interesting that what I remember most about my early years in athletics are the embarrassing incidents, dropping a ball on a crucial play at the plate, missing easy baskets or striking out with the bases loaded. Reading old newspaper clips as I have done for this book has reminded me of some of the more positive moments.

While working in Public Affairs for Ford Motor Company, I arranged and participated in more than 300 news conferences or other news media activities, yet the two events that stand out most prominently in my mind were embarrassing failures. The first was a news conference and demonstration of an air bag deployment in Austin I had arranged for a Ford vice president. The speech was prepared, a couple dozen chairs were in place and the microphone had been checked and double checked. Sweating nervously, I finally, reluctantly, stepped up to the microphone to introduce the vice president, as a lone reporter sat in the back row picking his teeth.

At another time, I invited the news media in New Orleans to interview the Lincoln-Mercury general sales manager in his hotel suite on the occasion of a new car introduction. Every few minutes I would peer down the hall desperately searching for any sign of life. No one showed. It was a shut out. We grabbed our bags and left for the airport. Strange that I should remember these two episodes and only faintly recall the successful ones.

As a youngster at William Ford school I can recall several incidents that relate to self esteem. On one occasion our class was sent single file to the nurse's office to be weighed. Elaine Fields was recording the weight of each person as we stepped on the scale. When my turn came, she announced my weight and commented that Jerry Lynch was the only boy in the class lighter than me. When I expressed my disappointment she turned to me and said, "Why do you want to be the lightest boy in the class? That's nothing to be proud of." I didn't answer. I didn't have an answer. I suppose I was desperate to receive some form of recognition

Following a card game in Pat McEvoy's basement in the summer of 1953 several friends talked about going off to college and what the future might hold for us. At the time I had no plans to go to college and was earning a few dollars an hour working for the Dearborn Recreation Department. "We're all friends now and should remain so throughout college and afterward," someone in the group said. "We need to hang together and should we ever be in a position to help another with a job, we should make a pact to do so." We shook hands. I thought this is one hell of a deal for me. I won't be in a position to help them, but it's good to know I can call on them should the need arise. ◆

14

DENNIS BALLOU and the
WRECKING CREW

"Everything in life is someplace else, and you get there in a car."

E.B. White

Dennis Ballou was a big man. He played football for Fordson high school during the early 50s, and while his career in that sport was less than distinguished, it wasn't from lack of size.

His father owned a neighborhood bar on Schaefer Road just one block from the high school. Among those who frequented the establishment was a sometimes construction worker named Red whose appetite for alcohol far exceeded his pocketbook. Over the course of a year or so Red's tab had reached several hundred dollars, a sum he was never likely to pay.

When Mr. Ballou confronted Red with a pay up or stay out ultimatum, Red reached in his pocket, grabbed the keys to his 1947 Ford and tossed them to Mr. Ballou. While the car was in bad need of repair and worth much less than Red owed, Mr. Ballou accepted the offer knowing his options were limited — it was the car or nothing.

Mr. Ballou was a successful bar keep whose taste ran more to late model Cadillacs than it did to rusted, abused Fords. He gave the car to Dennis.

With a little imagination, a 17-year-old high school student can have more fun with an almost worthless set of wheels than he can with a car that causes heartburn every time a scratch appears. Dennis took no better care of the car than did its previous owner.

During a heavy downpour one summer afternoon, Dennis was seated with a few friends around a table at Loretta's Confectionery. A customer walked in, shook his umbrella, and announced that the car parked in front had its windows open and the seats were getting soaked. Dennis continued to sip his Coke and without looking up said, "You can't spoil a rotten egg." That was Dennis's philosophy.

The most memorable experience we had with that car occurred just a few weeks later. It was about 4:30 p.m. and several of us were sipping Cokes at Loretta's. I don't remember who came up with the idea, but it received immediate unanimous approval. We set our half-finished drinks on the table and dashed out the door, piled in the car and drove to my house where we picked up a sledge hammer. Dennis was careful to park his car so he could pull out forward — the car had long since lost reverse.

With the sledge hammer in the back seat, we proceeded to the corner of Michigan Avenue and Schaefer Road, the busiest intersection in the city of Dearborn. And it was the busiest time of day as the huge Ford Rouge complex, with 65,000 employees, was in the midst of a shift change. Literally hundreds of people were milling the sidewalks waiting for buses or out shopping.

Coughing and spewing white smoke, the car lurched forward and came to a stop at the intersection just as the light changed to red. Dennis leaned over and turned off the ignition. My brother Jack reached down in the back seat and grabbed the sledge hammer preparing to make his move. When the light changed, Dennis mashed on the starter, it sputtered and shook, but did not start as we knew it wouldn't. The ignition was off. Dennis continued to hit the starter, but the car just stood there like a vibrating pile of junk. Irate drivers behind us began honking their horns while those on the sidewalk were turning in our direction.

The time was right. Jack slid out of the back seat, sledge hammer in hand and walked casually to the front of the car. He stood there rocking the hammer back and forth like a pendulum, gaining momentum until over it came with a crushing blow across the hood. At the moment of impact, Dennis turned on the ignition, stepped on the starter and she rumbled to life.

Bystanders and motorists starred in startled amazement, puzzled over the bizarre manner by which the car started. Jack strolled back to the car, tossed in the sledge hammer and we drove off.

Dennis retired as chief of police in Oak Park, Michigan. ◆

15

DATING

"When I was very young, I kissed my first woman and smoked my first cigarette on the same day. Believe me, never since have I wasted any more time on tobacco."

Arturo Toscanini

I first saw my wife, June Hopka, when we both were in the eighth grade, she at Woodworth and I at Maples. My best friend, Jerry Lynch, took me one evening to Woodworth where she was participating in a musical program. Jerry was interested in June and pointed her out to me as we watched the program from the balcony. When I actually met her is questionable. Some say I was introduced to her at the canteen by Gary Gates, but June says we met during a party at Shirley Fenger's home. Being of sane mind, I say June's right.

I thought she was beautiful and very nice, but I had struck up a relationship with another Woodworth girl, Harlean Ayres, and anyway June was sort of going with Jerry. We were invited to a Christmas party at the home of Shirley Fenger whose house was across the street from Woodworth. Jerry and I shopped together for gifts to exchange with our "dates" and settled on identical silk scarfs. When they opened their gifts, the girls were not too pleased to see they had received identical gifts, but Jerry and I sat there oblivious to their consternation and very proud of our purchase.

A few months later I parted company with Harlean and started dating June. We dated off and on until we were married on August 2, 1958. I recall on one occasion when we had broken off our relationship she went to the senior prom with my brother Jack. I didn't own a car until two years out of high school, and with a brother and two sisters vying for one car, June and I often walked to the show or to dances at Fordson.

Before Harlean and June, there were a few other infatuations dating back as early as elementary school. Jackie Denaro was a classmate who Jerry

Lynch and I would walk home from the ice rink on Chase Road. Joyce Battistone was another classmate who I thought was cute, but when Jerry Lynch would ask her if she liked me first or second, the answer was always second. One summer I met Dennis Doran's cousin, Arlene, who was visiting from East Detroit. I thought she was pretty nice, but what I remember most about her is that she had a beautiful voice and with a little encouragement would sing *Kisses Sweeter Than Wine*.

From the time we met until we were married, almost all of my dates were with June. Most of the time we just stayed home, usually at her house, and watched television. On Friday evenings her father would rush home from his Sunoco gas station in Garden City to watch the Friday Night Fights. The man worked seven days a week from 6 a.m. until 10 p.m. so those boxing matches were welcome relaxation. Every afternoon he would drive home for lunch, lie down for an hour and then drive to his 40-acre farm in Brownstown Township where he would feed his animals or work the fields before returning to the station. His wife Julia often would go to the station to clean windshields, a common practice before we had self service gas stations. June would help there, too, from time to time. After I bought my first car, a 1953 Mercury 4-door, we would drive to the station and sit around drinking coffee. She was a cheap date. Her dad might even change my oil and grease the car while we sat around chewing the fat.

On August 2, 1958, we were married at St. Clements church in Dearborn. Both my sisters also were married in 1958, Patty to Gene Schenk and Glenda to Tommy Bruce. Older brother Jack had already been discharged from the Army and was living in an apartment with Louis Zuzak. Youngest brother Tom was the only child still left at home.

Our wedding reception on August 2, 1958

Following our marriage, we went to New England for our honeymoon. When we returned, June's father was working the farm where we were to live. We stopped in the lane and he got off the tractor, welcomed us home and casually mentioned there was a letter for me on the kitchen table. It wasn't just any letter I discovered when it was opened. It was my draft notice. Two days later we had a farewell party and the next day I was inducted into the Army at Ft. Wayne and shipped off to Fort Knox for basic training.

In the Army at Ft. Lewis, Washington

Eight weeks later June came to visit me at Ft. Knox and informed me she was pregnant with our first child, Todd. I was thrilled, but it occurred to me then that if we had been married a month earlier, or I had been drafted a month later, I would not have had to go into the service. A married man with a child or pregnant wife was exempt from the draft. Anyway, as much as I disliked the Army, it was a maturing experience. ◆

16

LATER, MANY YEARS LATER

Mom and her kids (back row from left) Glenda Bruce, mom, Patty Schenk, (front row) Jack, Tom and me.

My family (from left), Randy, Todd, June, me, Michelle Kaufmann and Eric.

ABOUT THE AUTHOR

Bob Bierman retired from Ford Motor Company in 1995 following a 41-year career in public relations. He joined the Company in 1953 as a tour guide at the Ford Rotunda. At the time of his retirement he directed public relations activities for the Company in the 13-state Western Region. His mother still lives in the home in Dearborn, MI.,where he was raised and received his early formal education. He graduated from Wayne State University in Detroit in 1963. He is married to the former June Hopka. They live in Tellico Village, TN, and have four grown children.